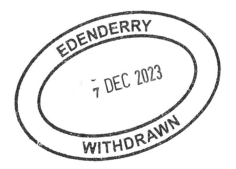

TO: _____

FROM: _____

I JUST WANTED TO SAY

_____

_____

_____

ABOUT THE AUTHOR

ROB STEARS IS AN ILLUSTRATOR LIVING
IN DUBLIN WITH HIS WIFE AND SON.

HE STARTED DOODLING AT AN EARLY AGE AND
HAS YET TO STOP.

SEE MORE AT ROBSTEARS.IE

WHY I LOVE MY MUM

A CELEBRATION OF THE ONE WHO MAKES THE WORLD GO ROUND

ROB STEARS

HACHETTE
BOOKS
IRELAND

First published in 2017 by Hachette Books Ireland

A CIP catalogue record for this title is available from the British Library.

ISBN 978 1 47366 084 7

Typesetting by redrattledesign.com
Printed and bound in Great Britain by Clays , St Ives plc.

Hachette Books Ireland's policy is to use papers that are natural, renewable and recyclable and made from wood grown in sustainable forests. The logging and manufacturing processes are expected to conform to the environmental regulations of the country of origin.

Hachette Books Ireland
8 Castlecourt Centre
Castleknock
Dublin 15, Ireland

A division of Hachette UK Ltd
Carmelite House, Victoria Embankment,
London EC4Y 0DZ
www.hachettebooksireland.ie

CONTENTS

FOR ANNE AND ADAM

MY MUM IS MY BIGGEST FAN

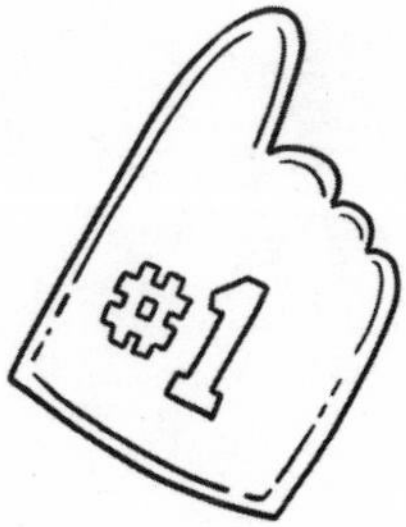
#1

SCHOOL PLAY
SUCH TALENT! WHAT A PERFORMANCE!
THANKS MUM

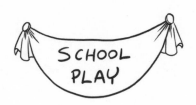

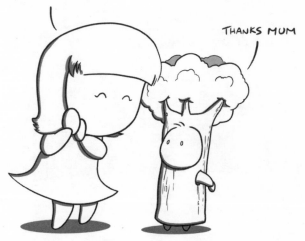

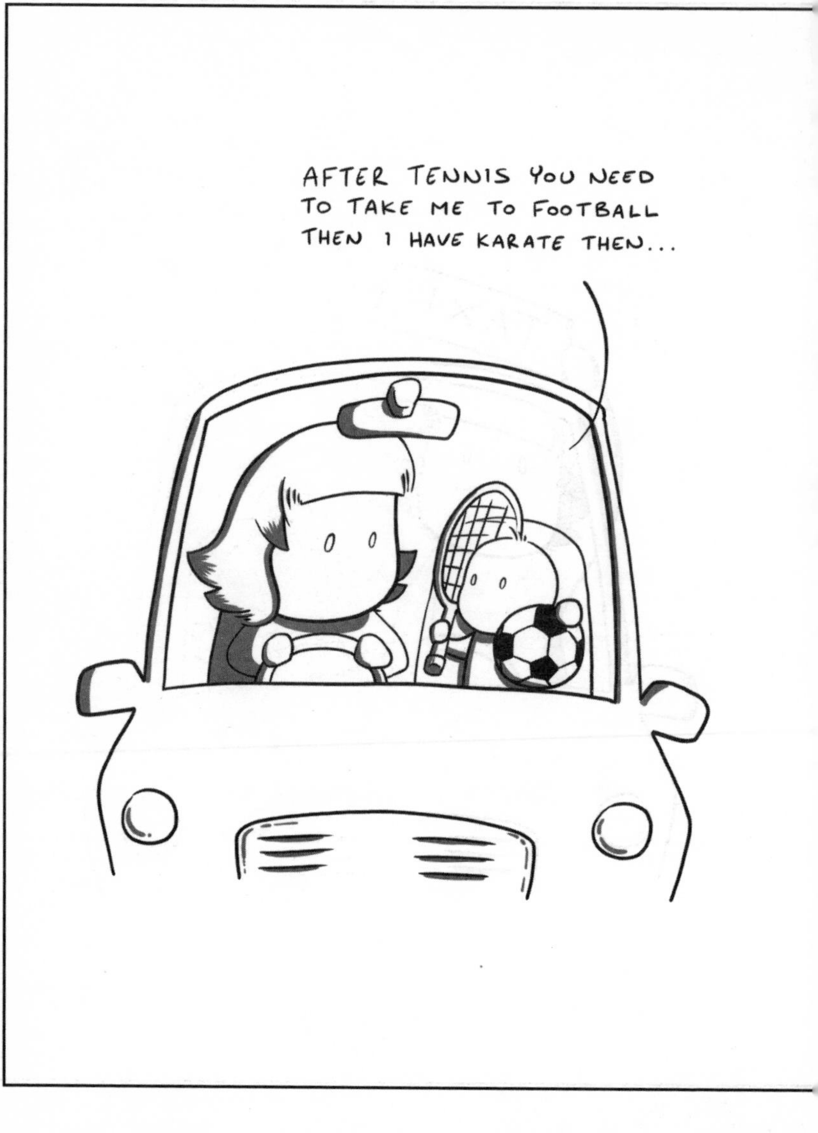
AFTER TENNIS YOU NEED TO TAKE ME TO FOOTBALL THEN I HAVE KARATE THEN...

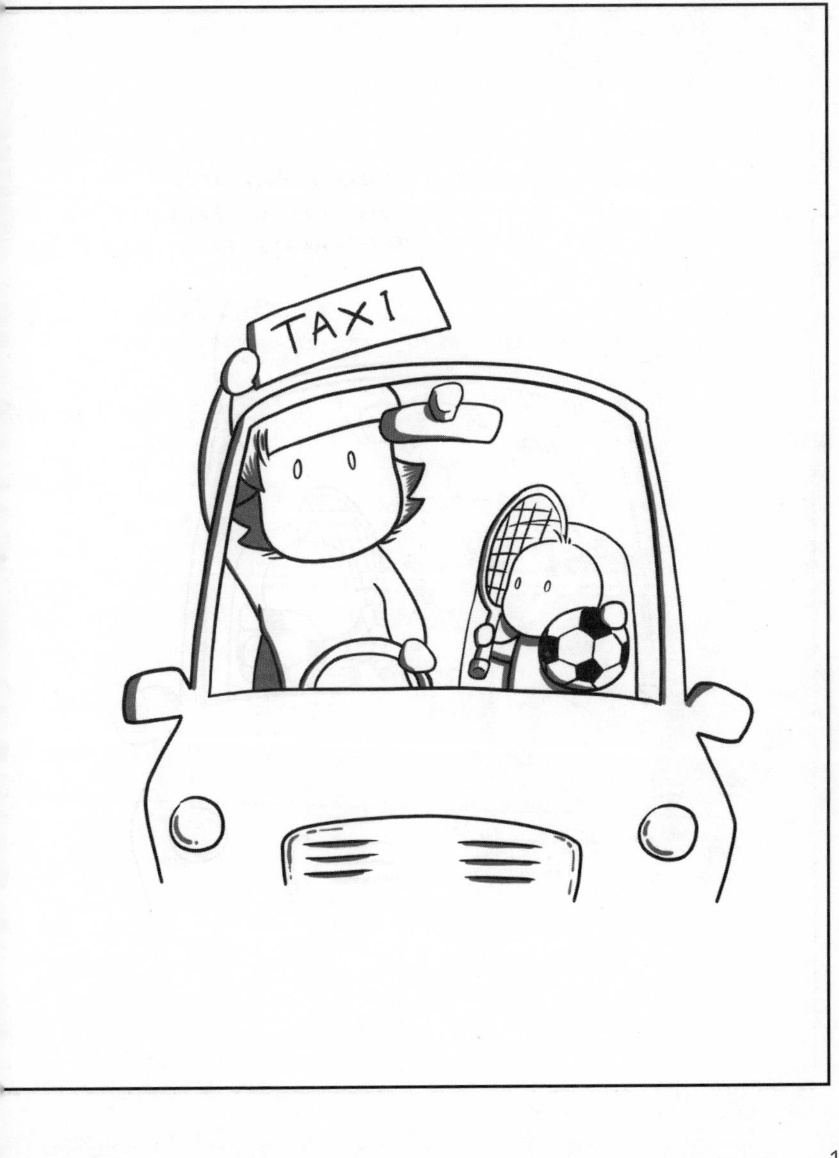
TAXI

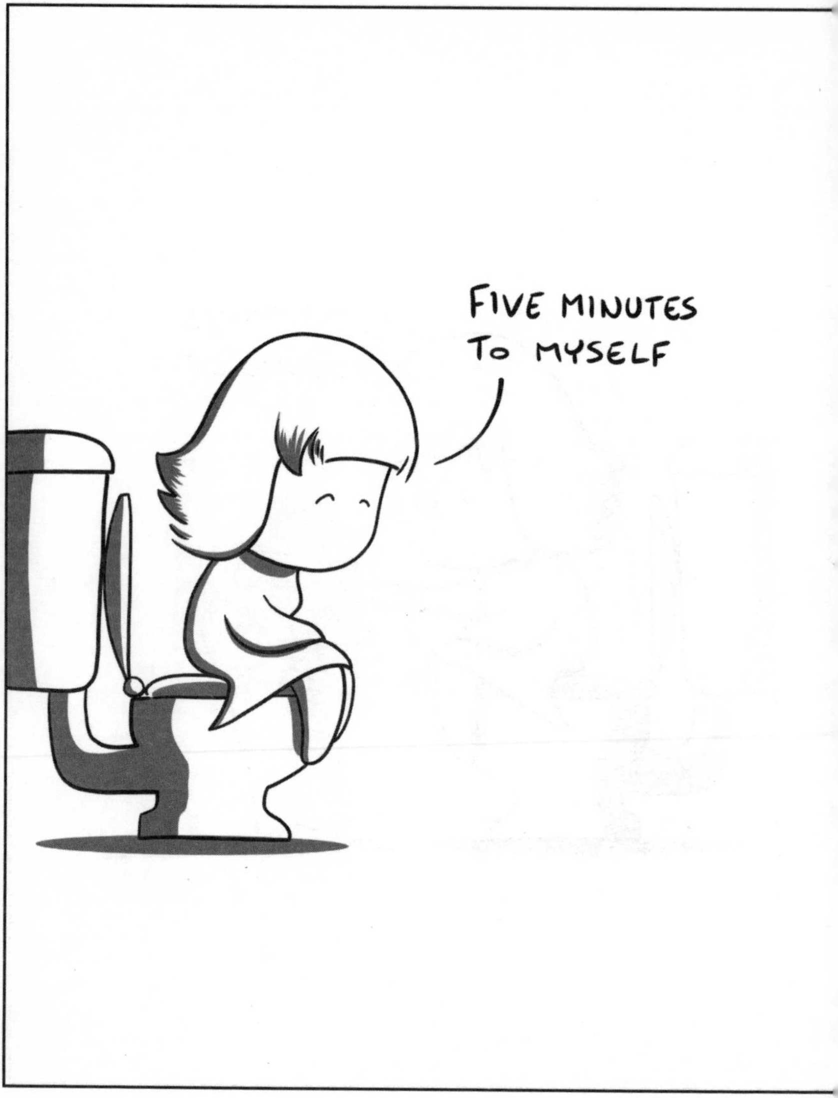
FIVE MINUTES TO MYSELF

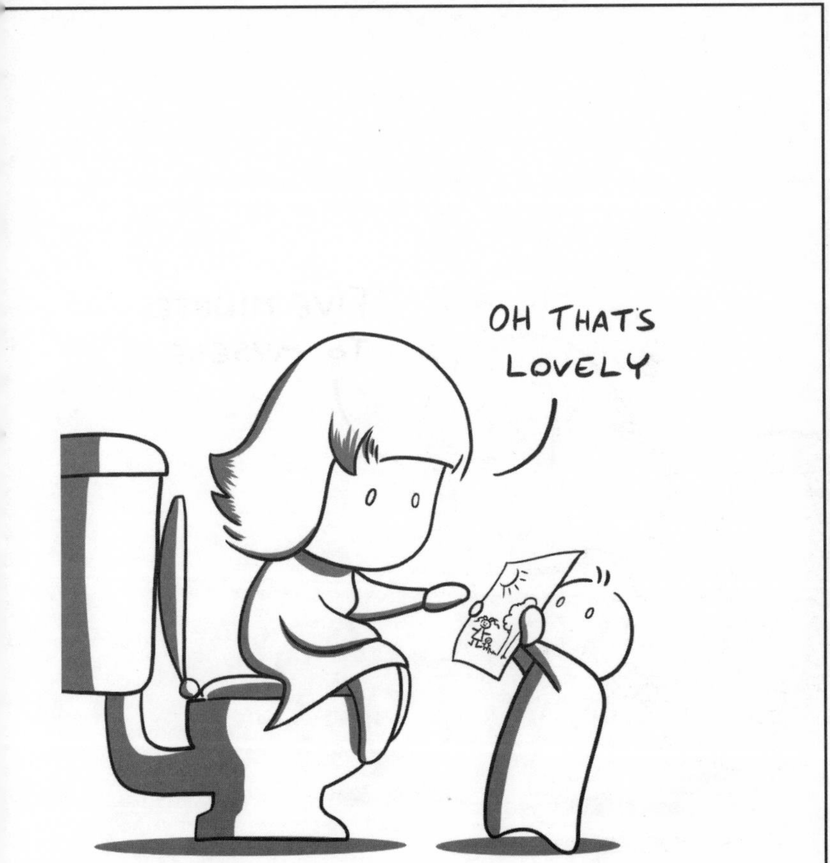
OH THAT'S LOVELY

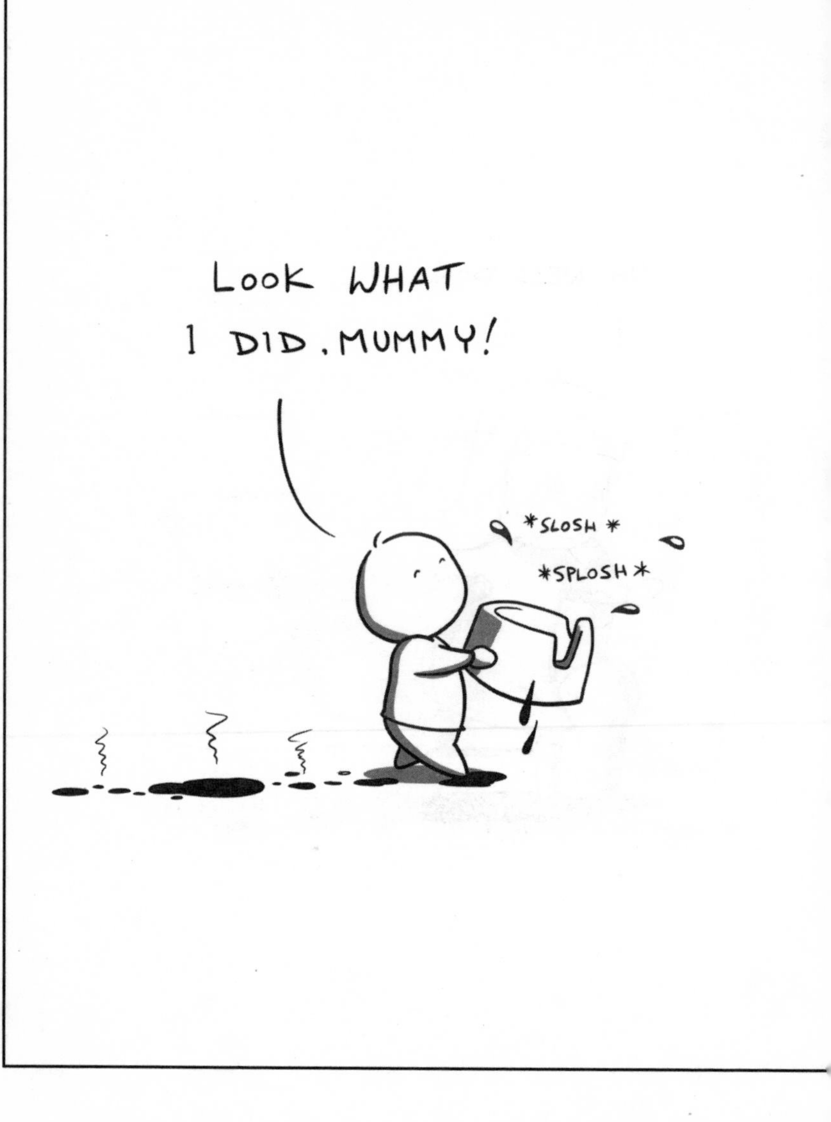
LOOK WHAT I DID, MUMMY!
SLOSH
SPLOSH

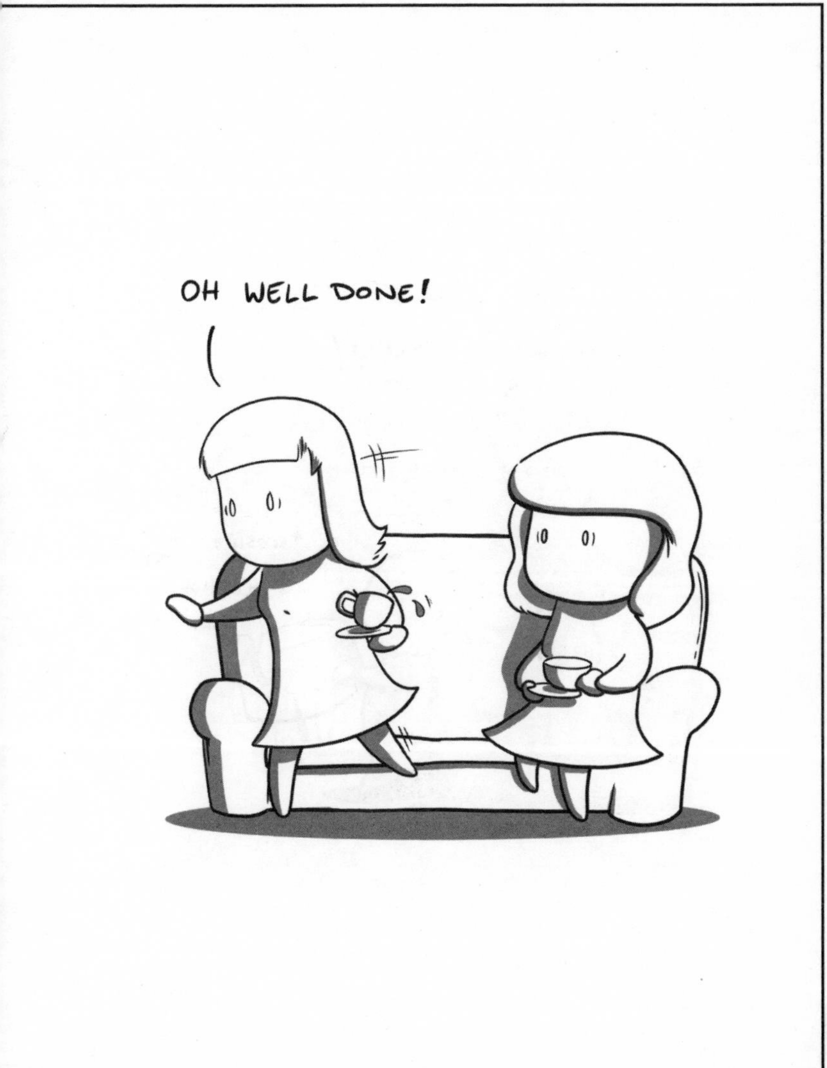
OH WELL DONE!

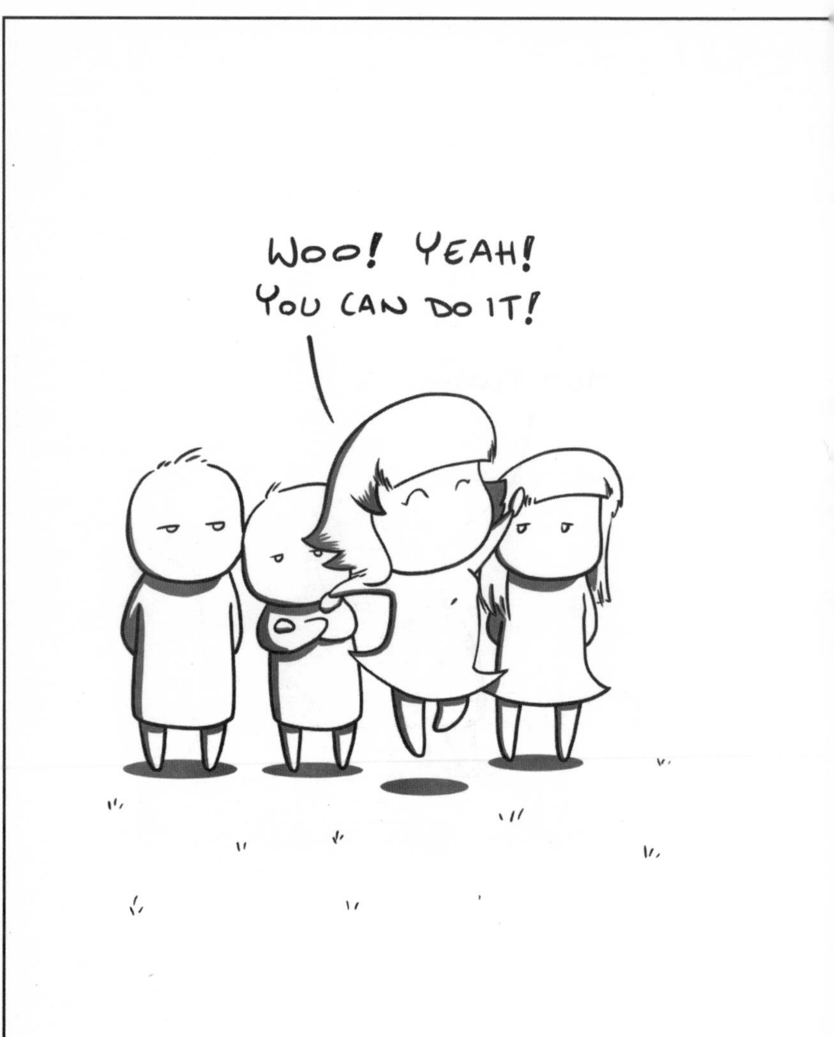
WOO! YEAH! YOU CAN DO IT!

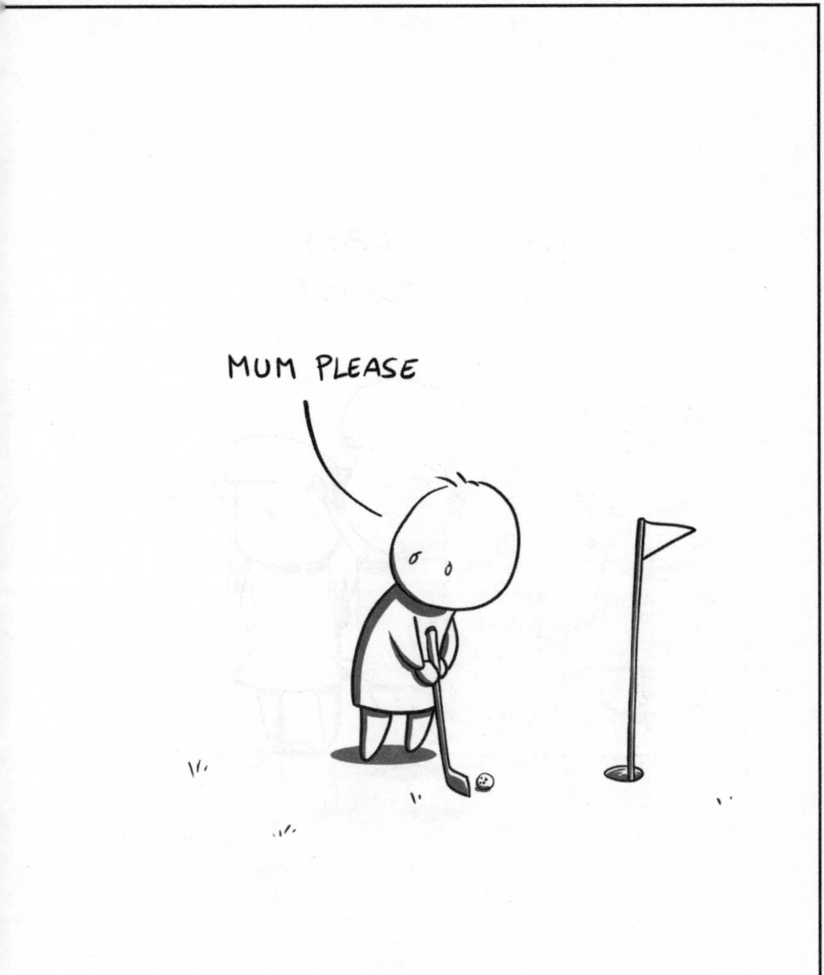
MUM PLEASE

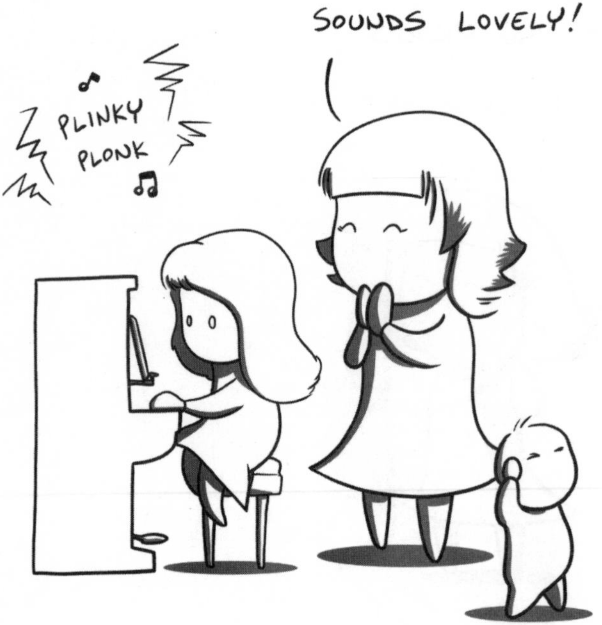
PLINKY
PLONK
SOUNDS LOVELY!

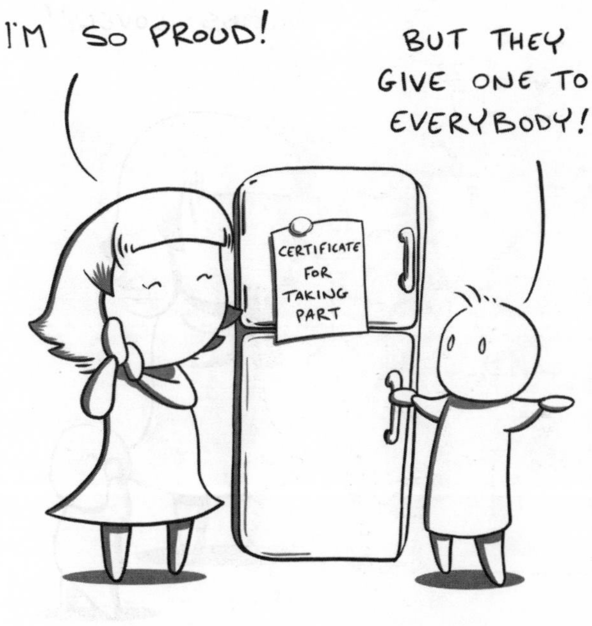
I'M SO PROUD!
BUT THEY GIVE ONE TO EVERYBODY!
CERTIFICATE FOR TAKING PART

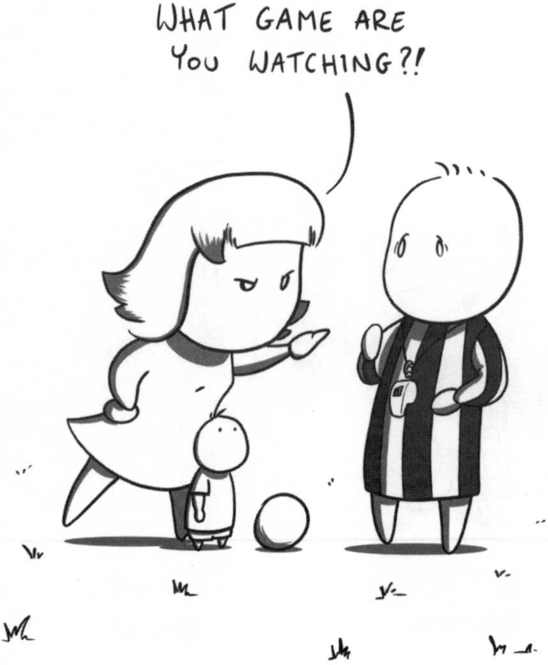
WHAT GAME ARE YOU WATCHING?!

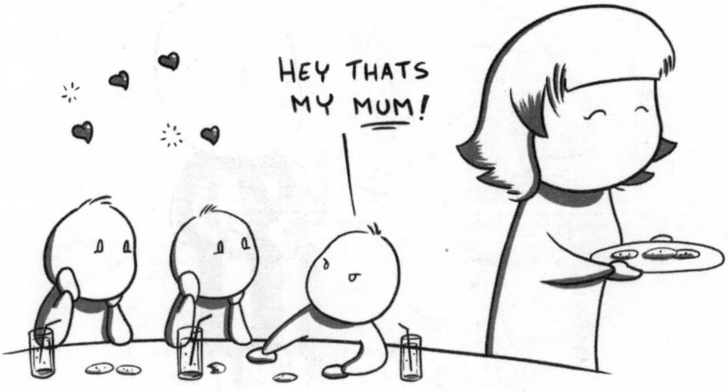
HEY THATS
MY MUM!

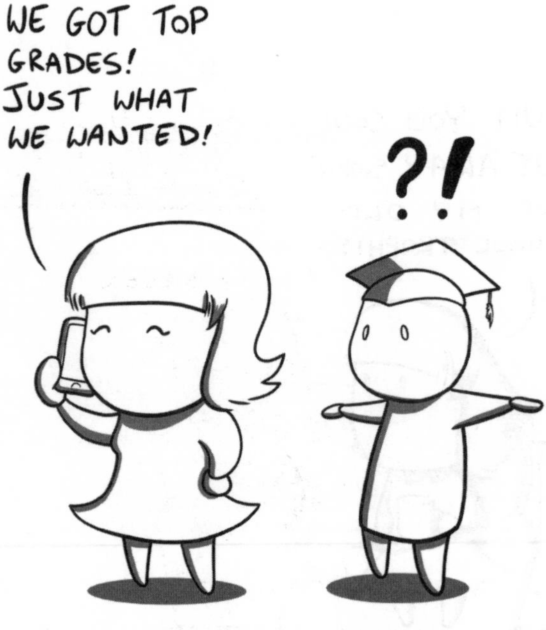
WE GOT TOP GRADES! JUST WHAT WE WANTED!
?!

MUM YOU COULD PUT AWAY SOME OF MY OLD SCHOOL TROPHIES

NEVER

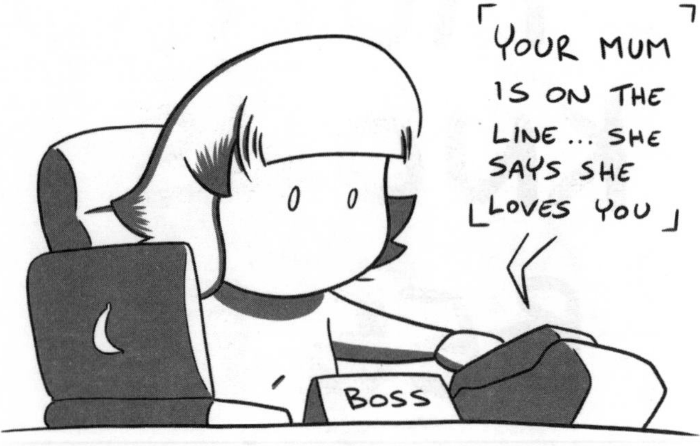
YOUR MUM IS ON THE LINE ... SHE SAYS SHE LOVES YOU
BOSS

MUM KNOWS BEST

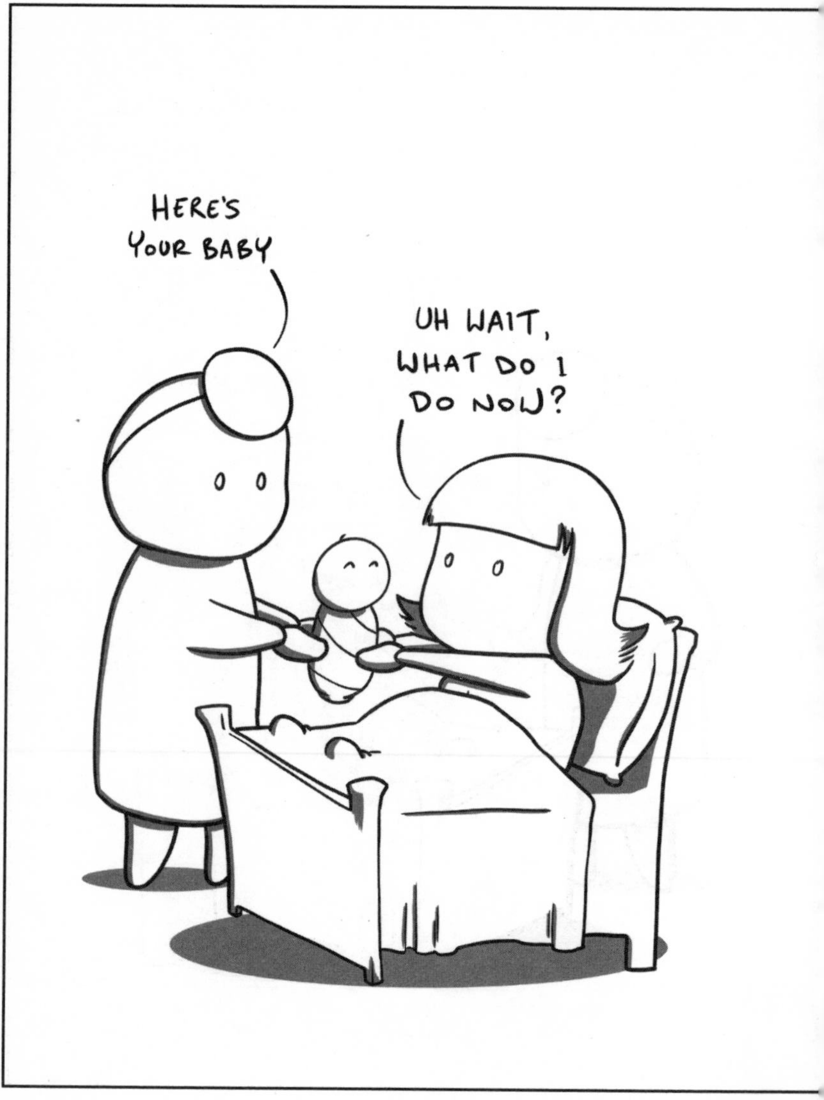
HERE'S YOUR BABY
UH WAIT, WHAT DO I DO NOW?

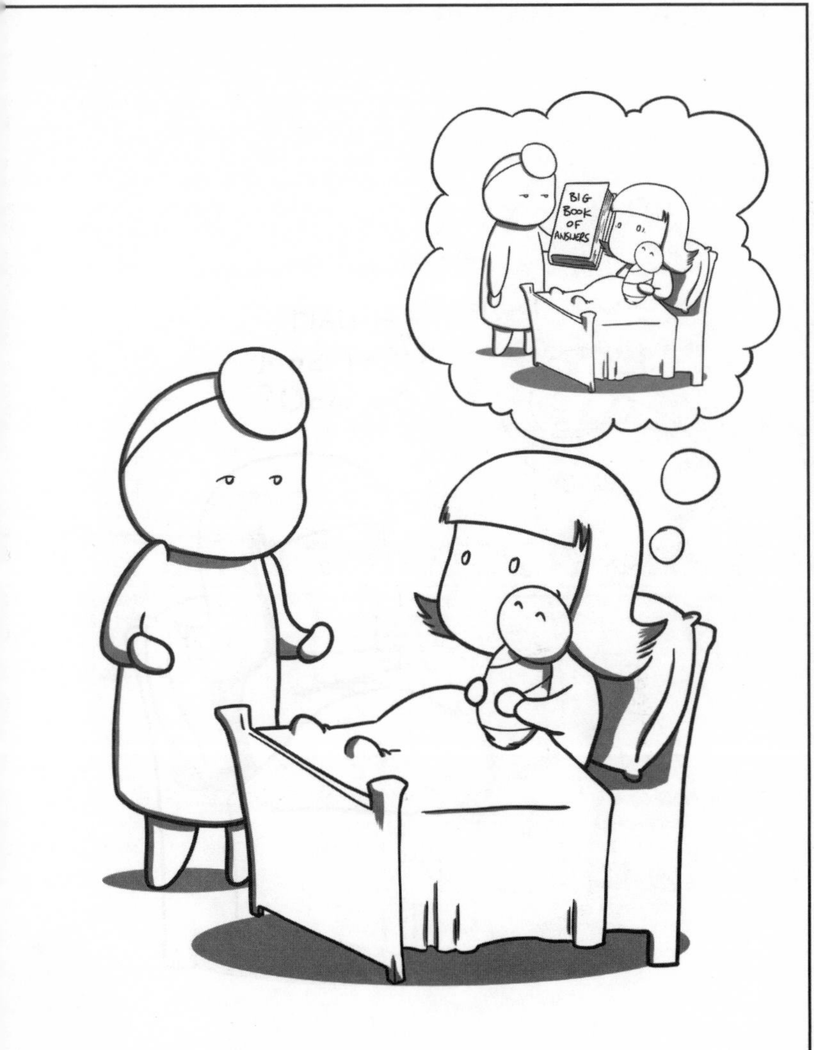
BIG
BOOK
OF
ANSWERS

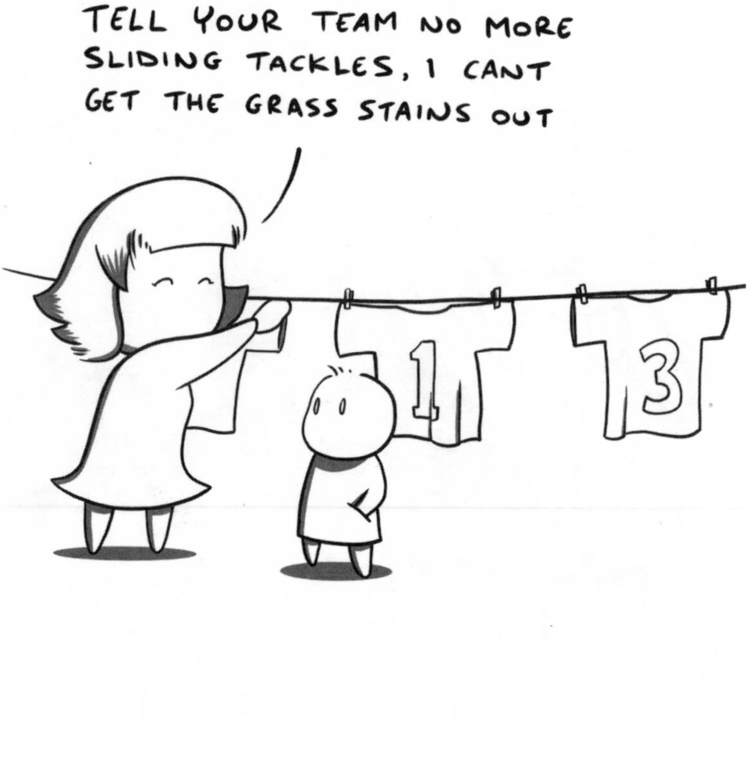
TELL YOUR TEAM NO MORE SLIDING TACKLES, I CANT GET THE GRASS STAINS OUT
1
3

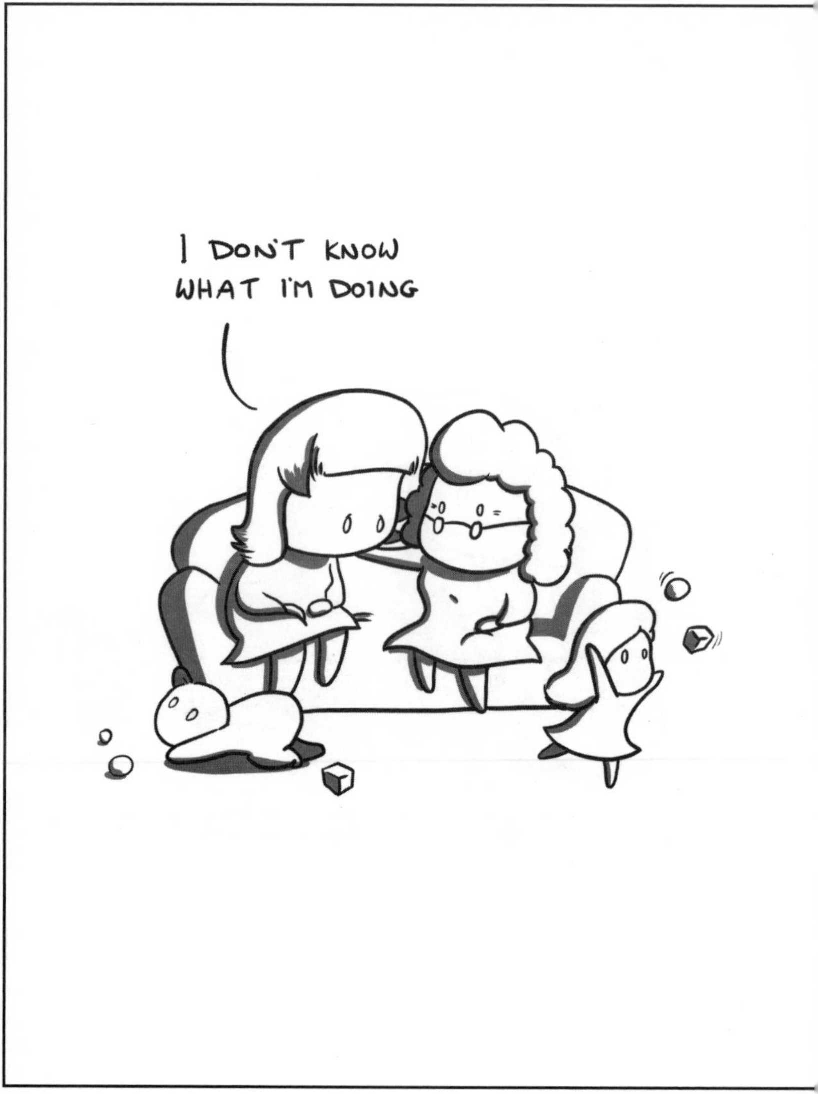
I DON'T KNOW WHAT I'M DOING

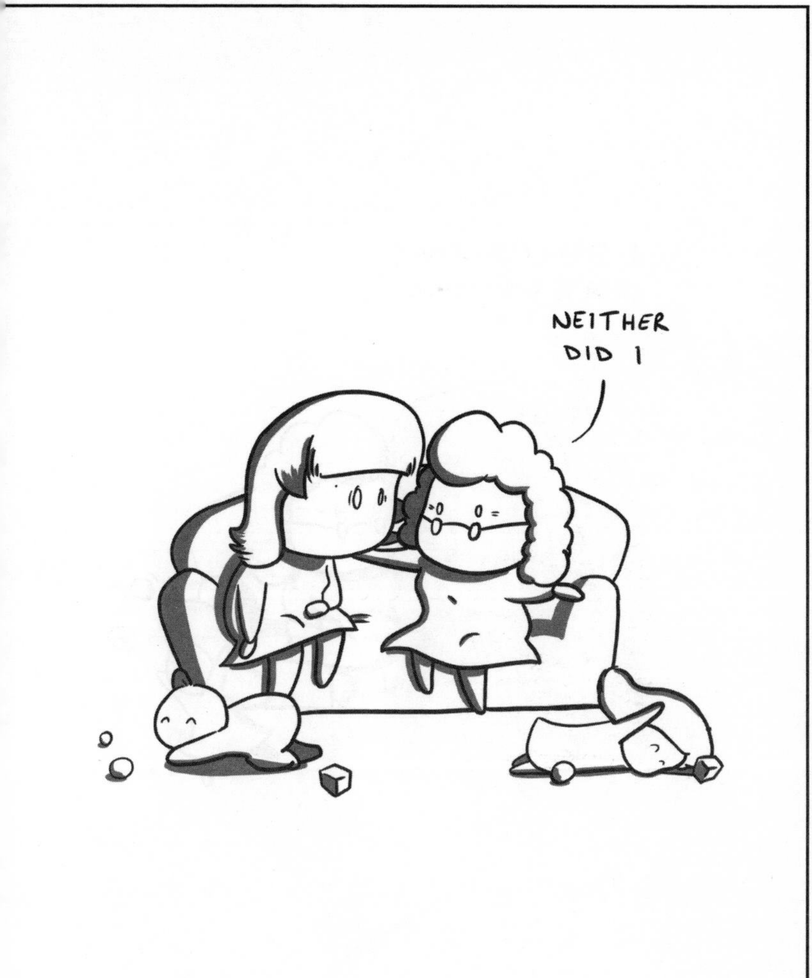
NEITHER DID I

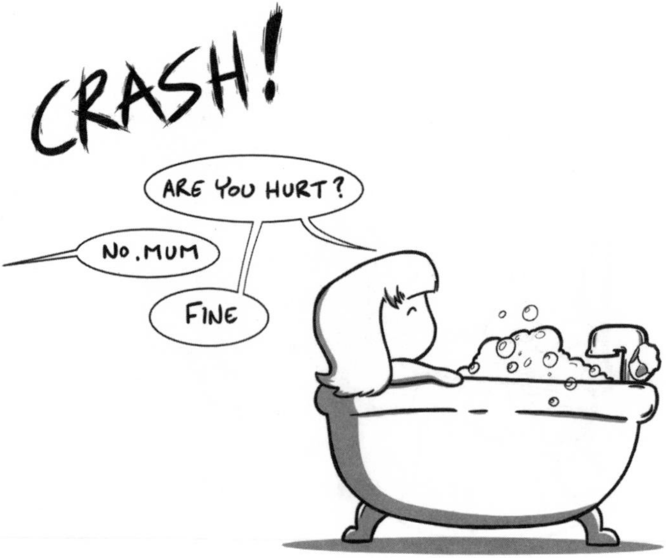
CRASH!
ARE YOU HURT?
NO. MUM
FINE

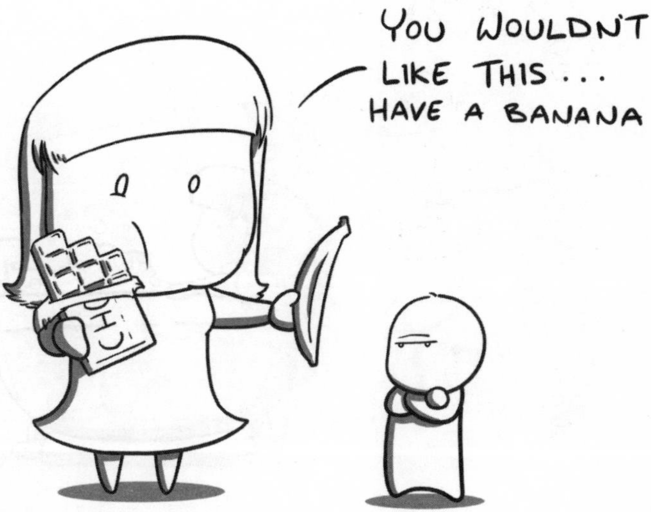
YOU WOULDN'T
LIKE THIS ...
HAVE A BANANA
CHO

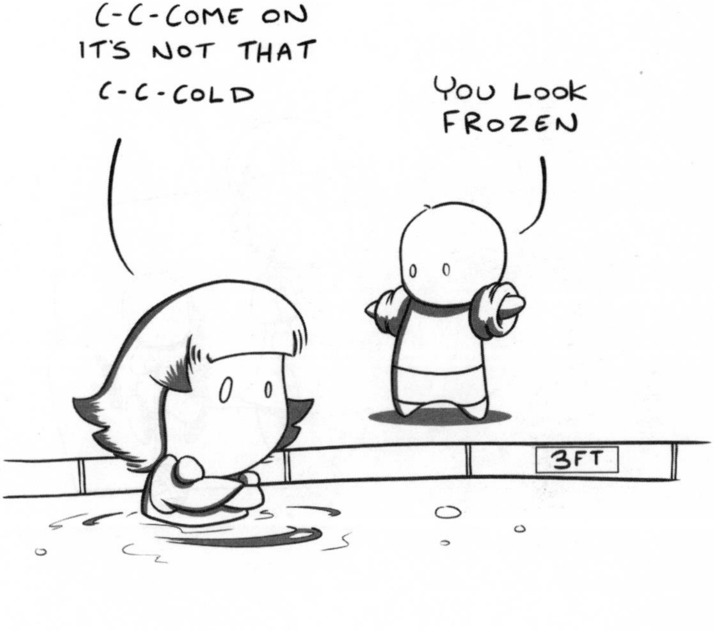
C-C-COME ON IT'S NOT THAT C-C-COLD
YOU LOOK FROZEN
3FT

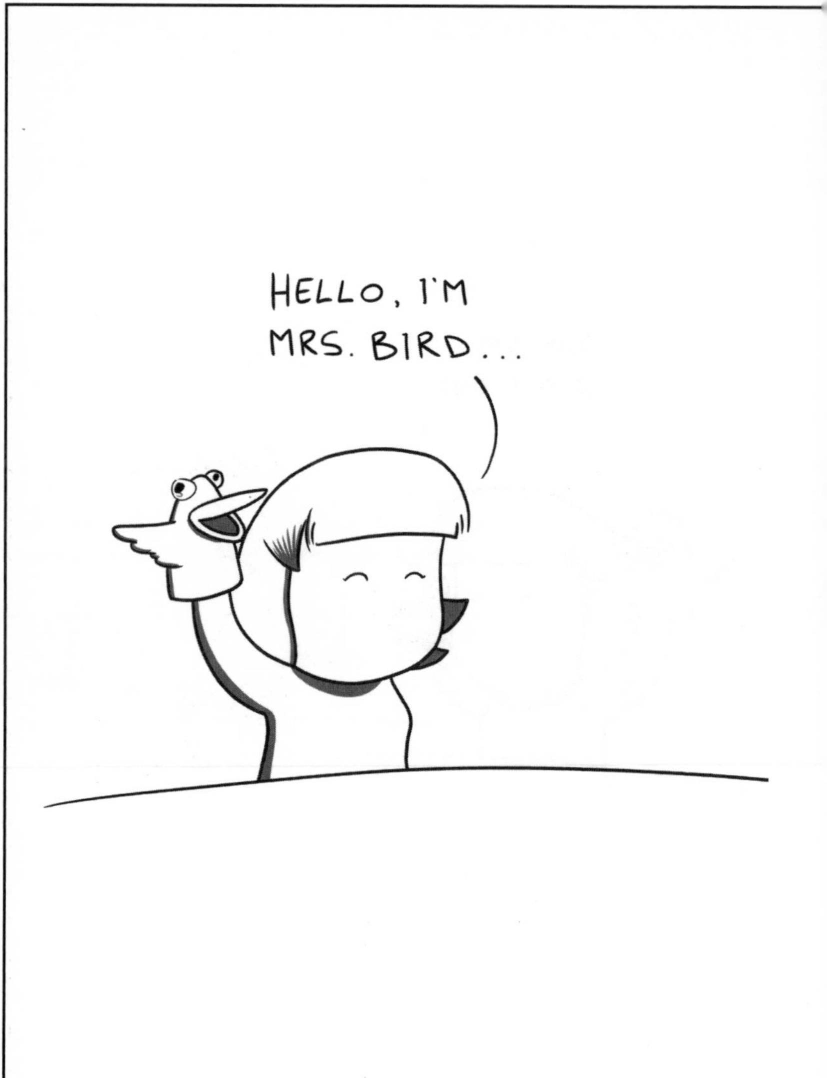
HELLO, I'M
MRS. BIRD...

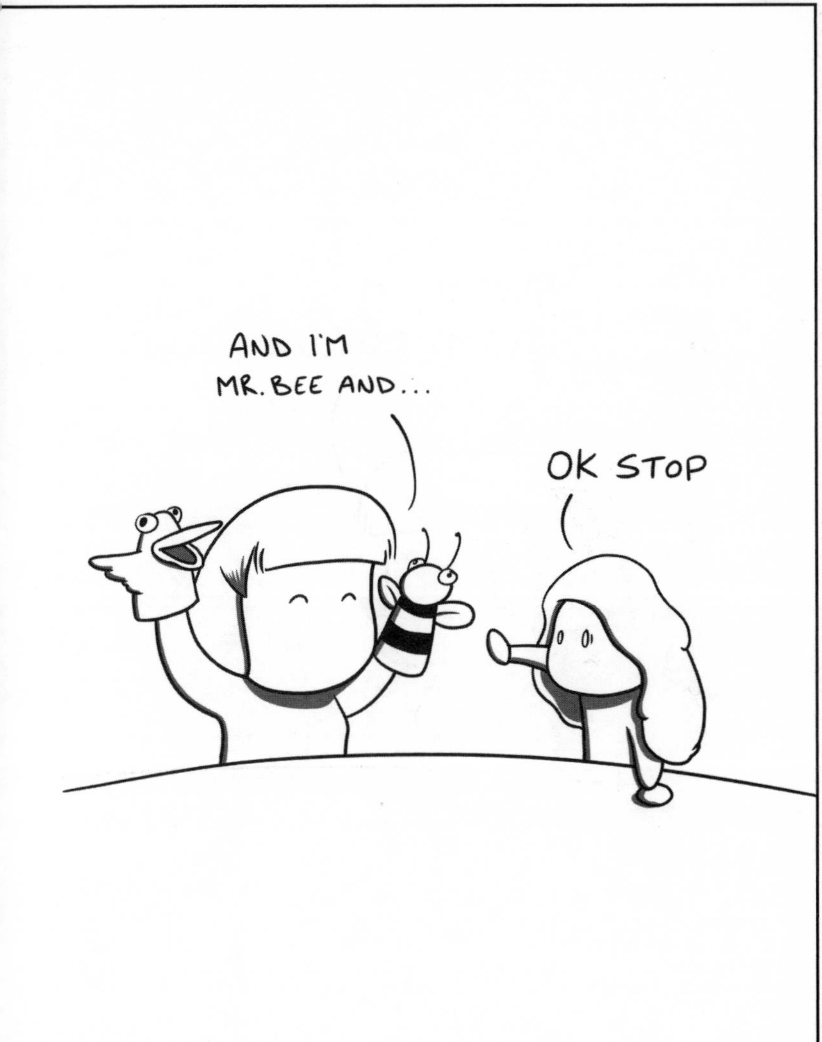
AND I'M
MR. BEE AND...
OK STOP

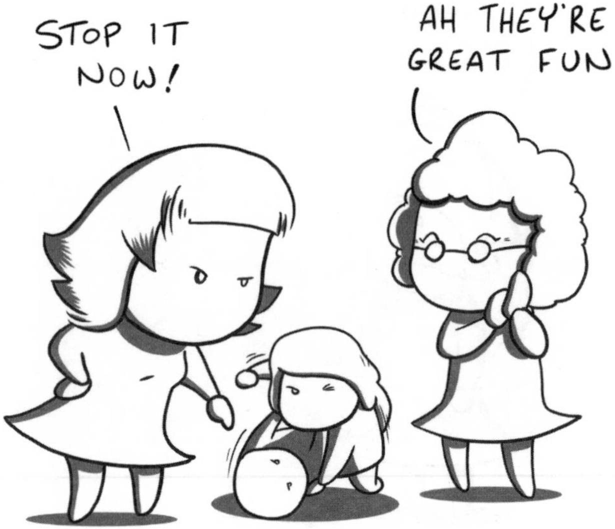
STOP IT NOW!
AH THEY'RE GREAT FUN

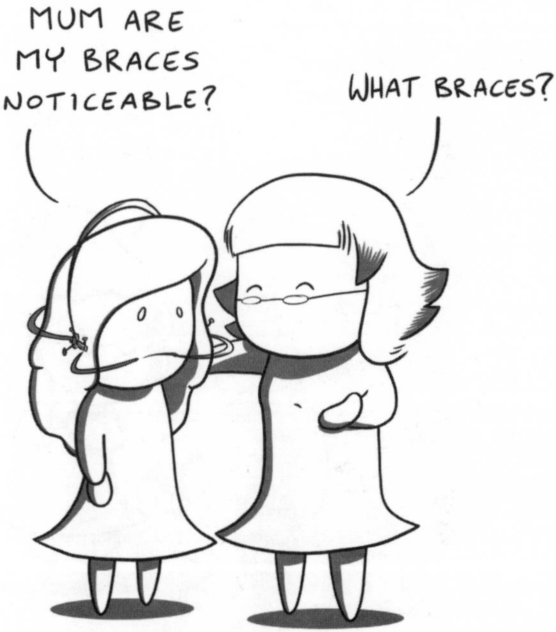
MUM ARE MY BRACES NOTICEABLE?
WHAT BRACES?

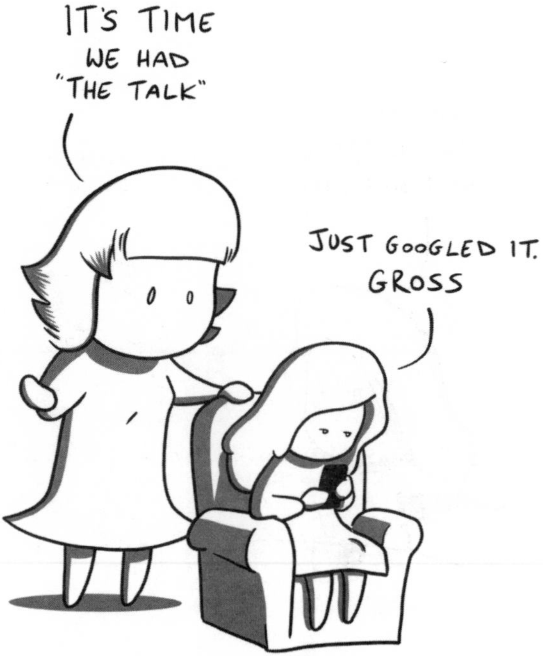
IT'S TIME WE HAD "THE TALK"
JUST GOOGLED IT. GROSS

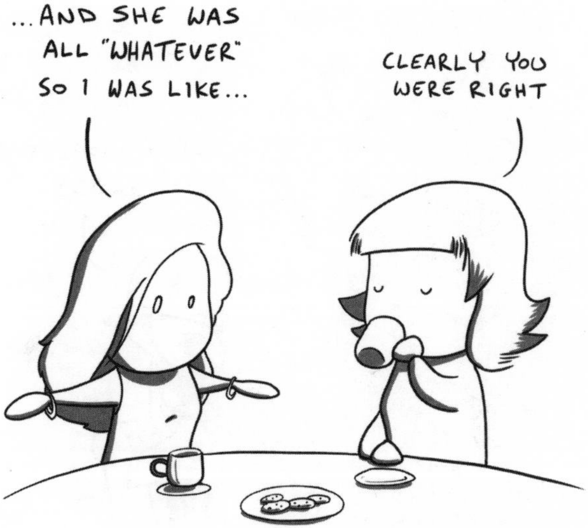
...AND SHE WAS ALL "WHATEVER" SO I WAS LIKE...
CLEARLY YOU WERE RIGHT

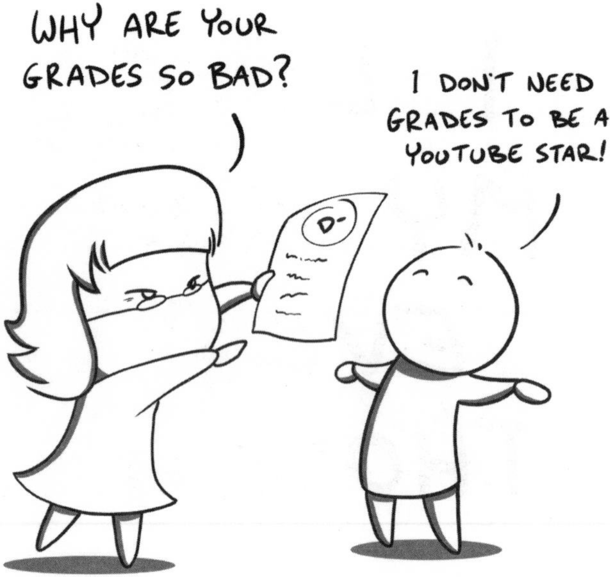
WHY ARE YOUR GRADES SO BAD?
D-
I DON'T NEED GRADES TO BE A YOUTUBE STAR!

I LOVE
MY MUM
EVEN
THOUGH...

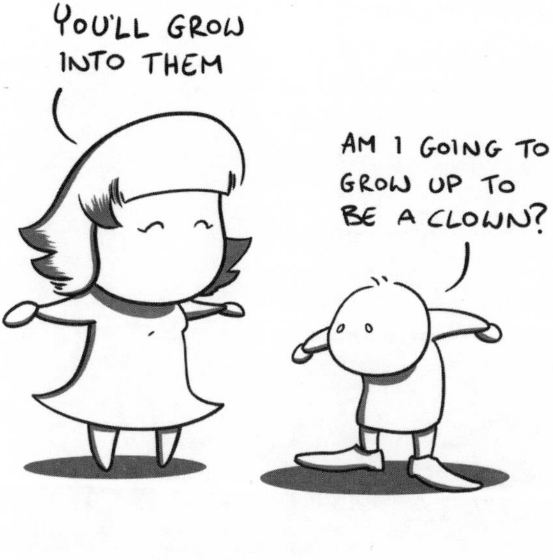
YOU'LL GROW INTO THEM
AM I GOING TO GROW UP TO BE A CLOWN?

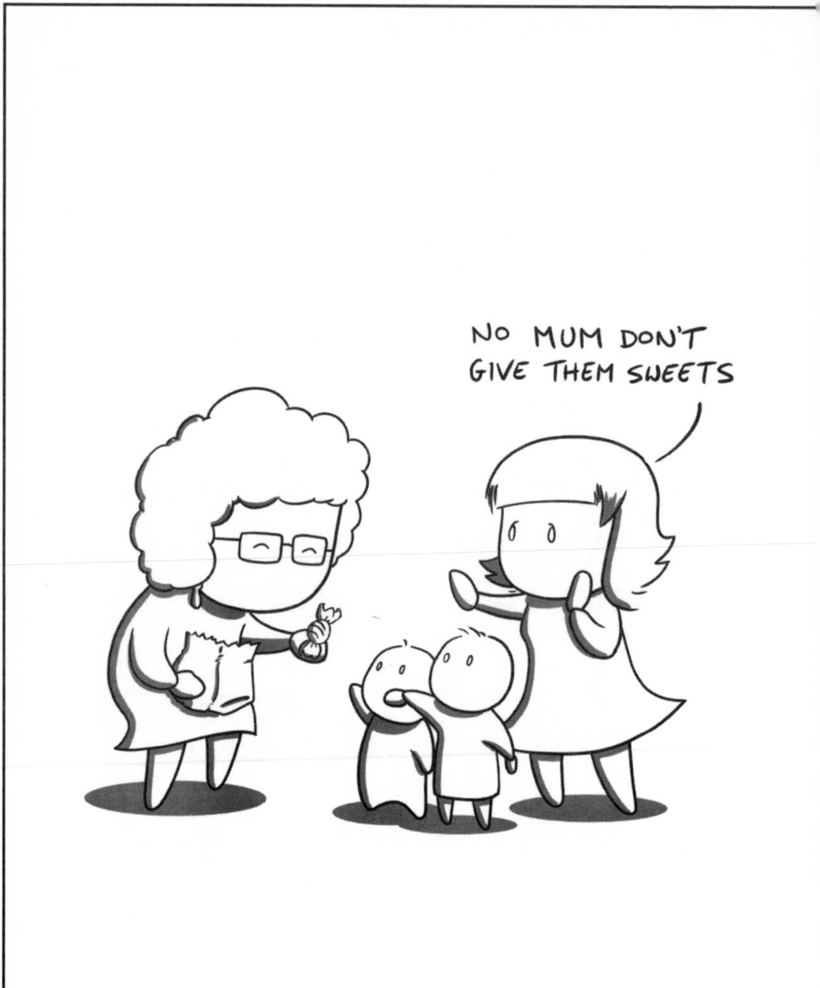
NO MUM DON'T
GIVE THEM SWEETS

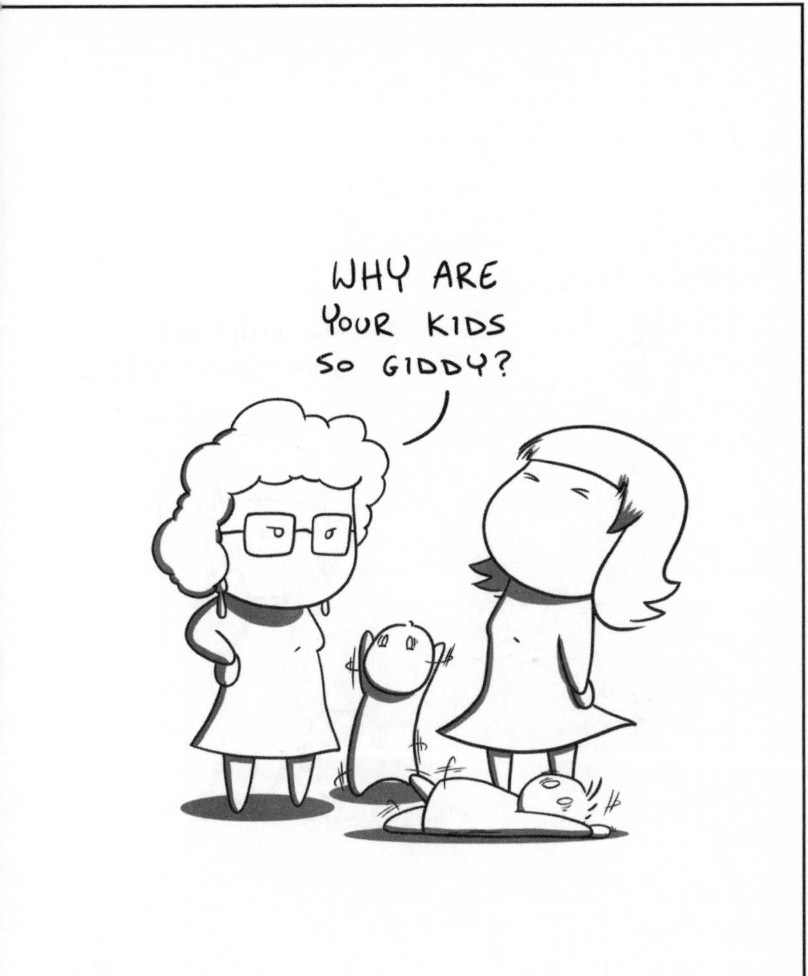
WHY ARE YOUR KIDS SO GIDDY?

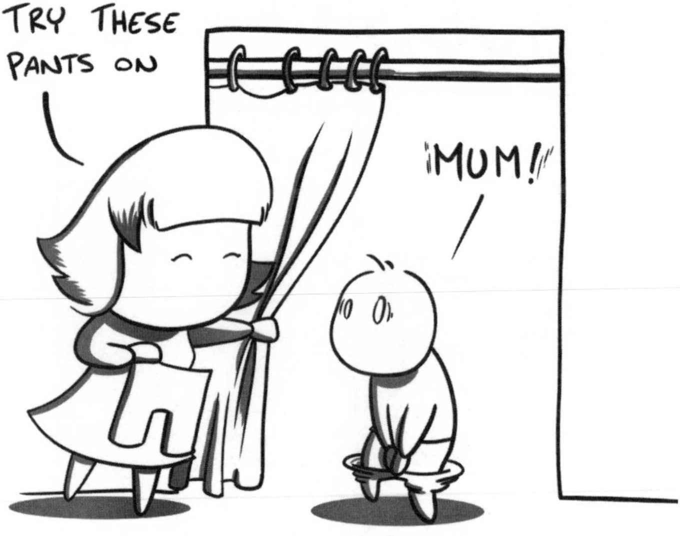
TRY THESE PANTS ON
¡MUM!

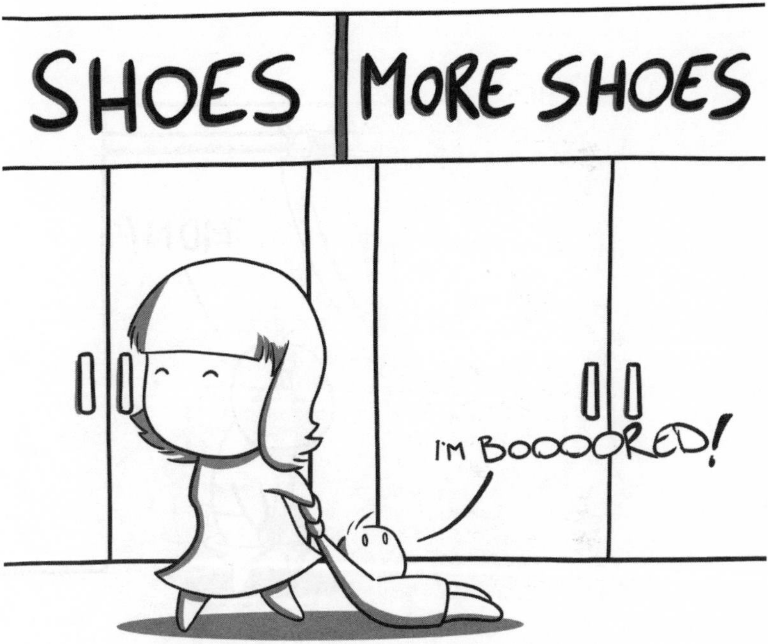
SHOES
MORE SHOES
I'M BOOOOORED!

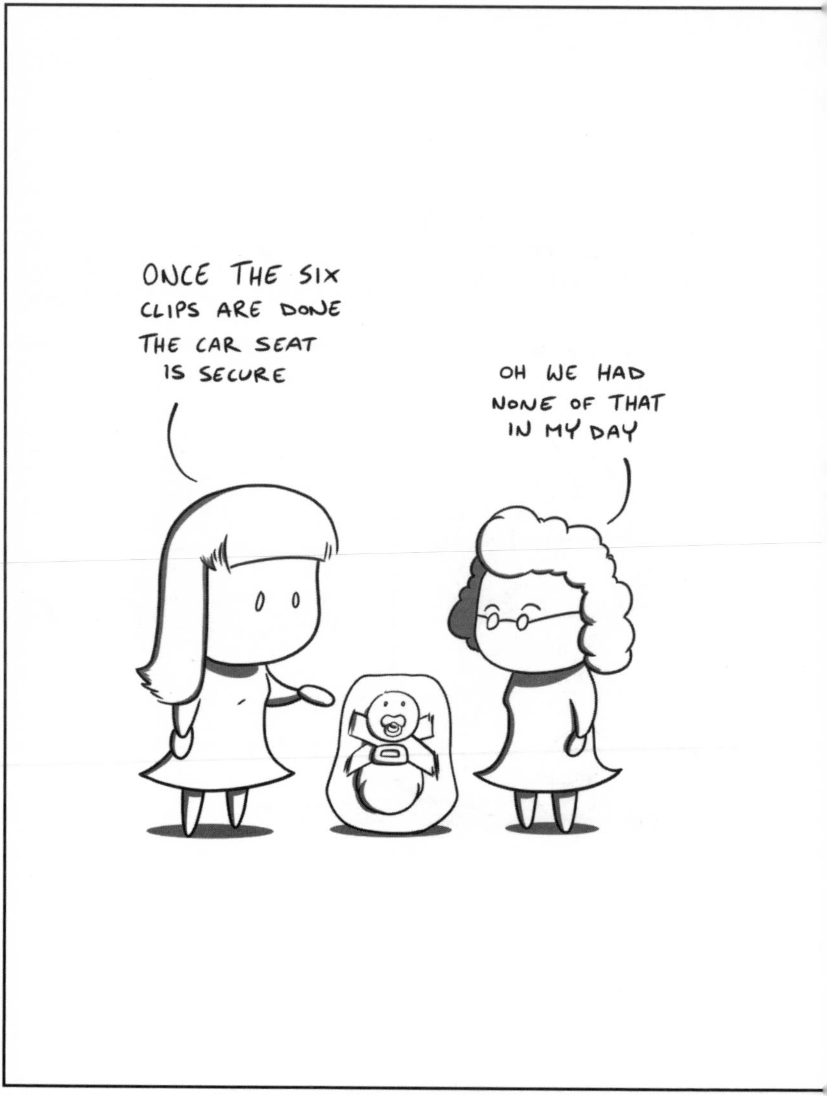
ONCE THE SIX CLIPS ARE DONE THE CAR SEAT IS SECURE
OH WE HAD NONE OF THAT IN MY DAY

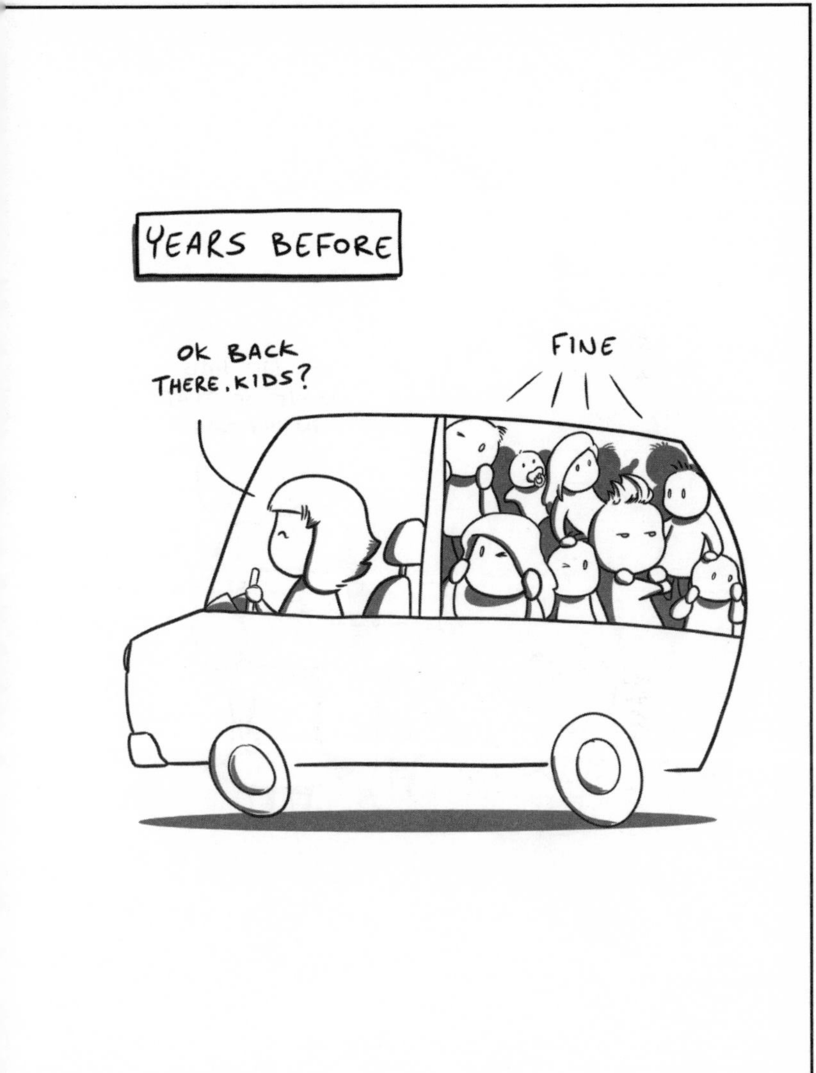
YEARS BEFORE
OK BACK THERE, KIDS?
FINE

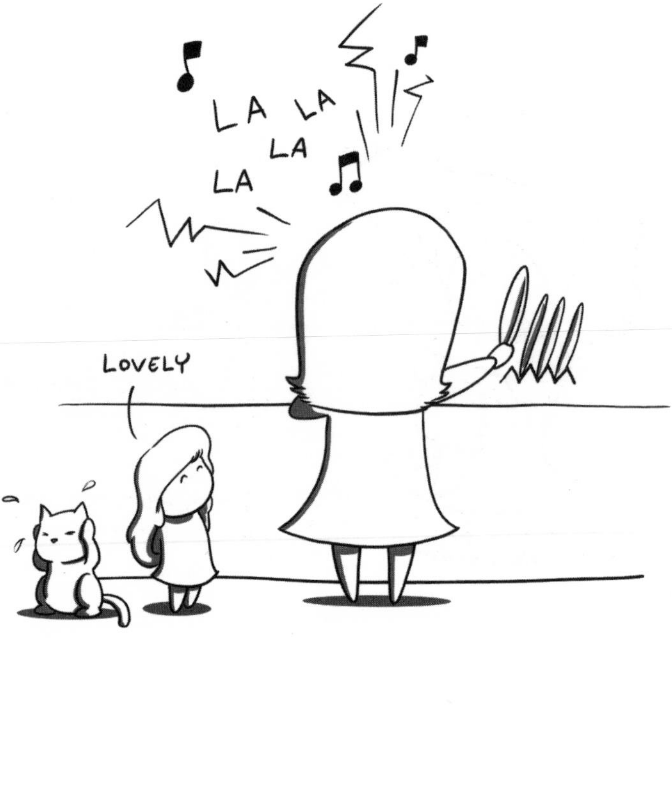
LA LA
LA
LA
LOVELY

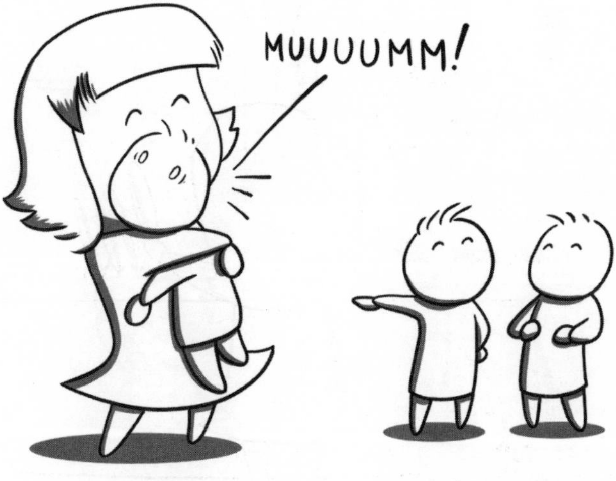
MUUUUMM!

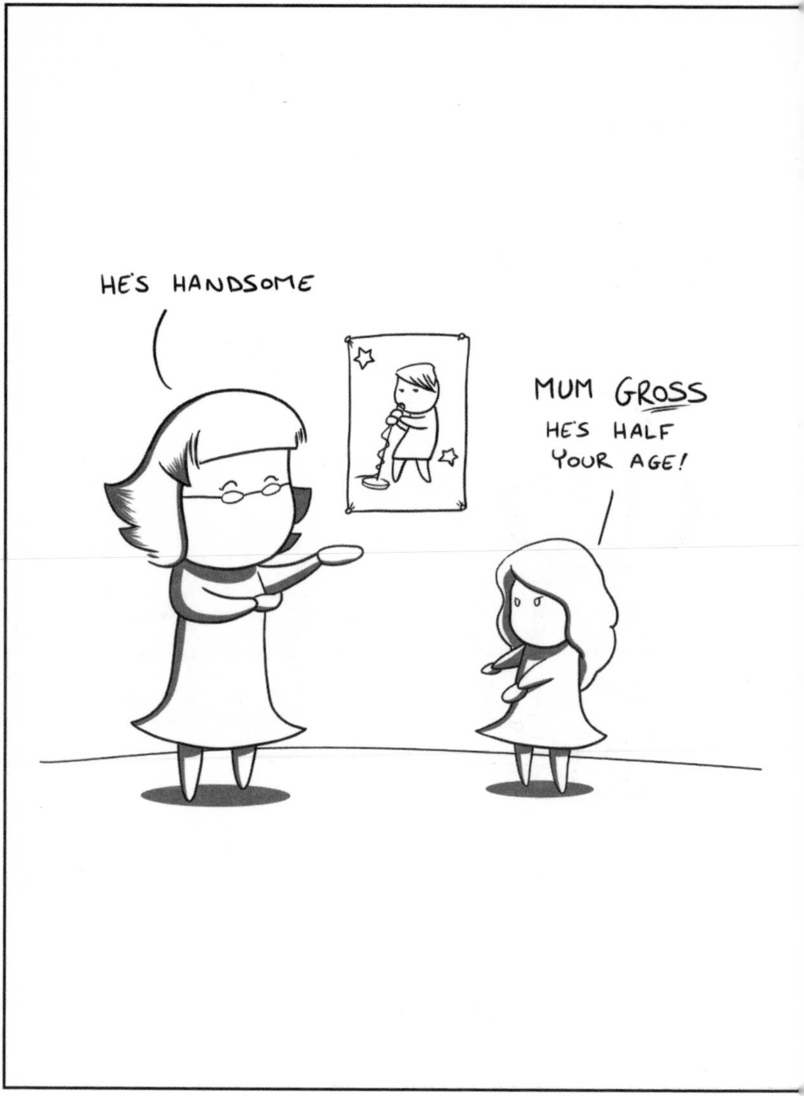
HE'S HANDSOME
MUM GROSS
HE'S HALF YOUR AGE!

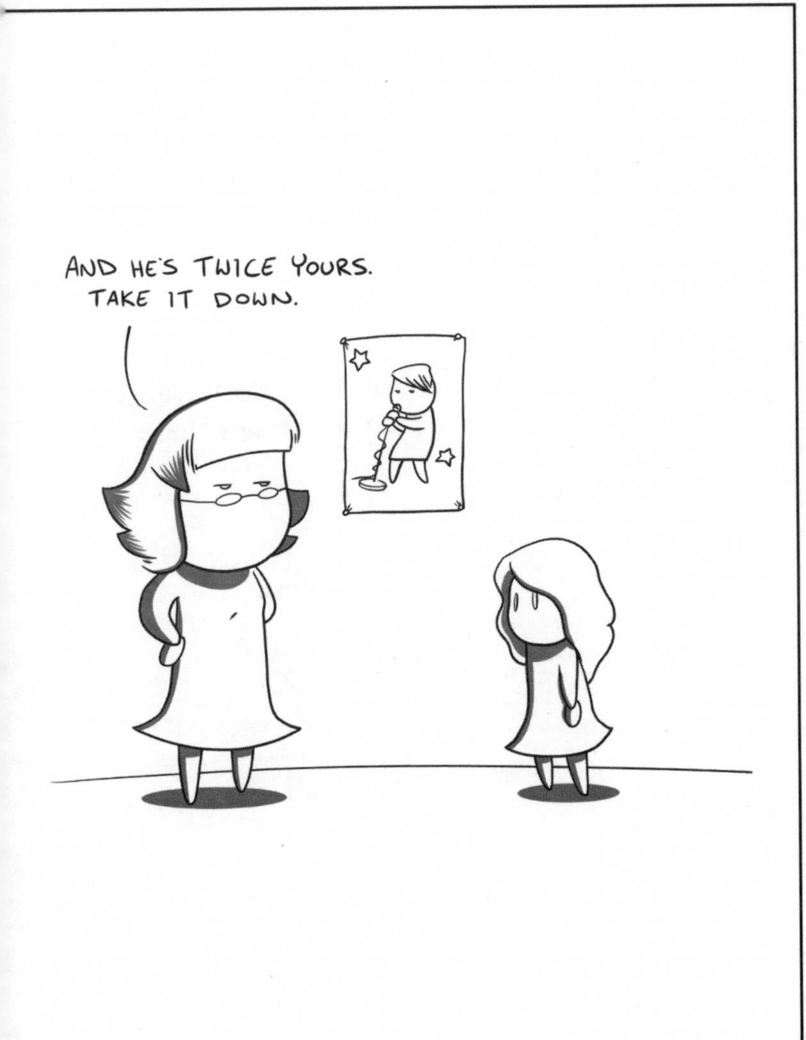
AND HE'S TWICE YOURS.
TAKE IT DOWN.

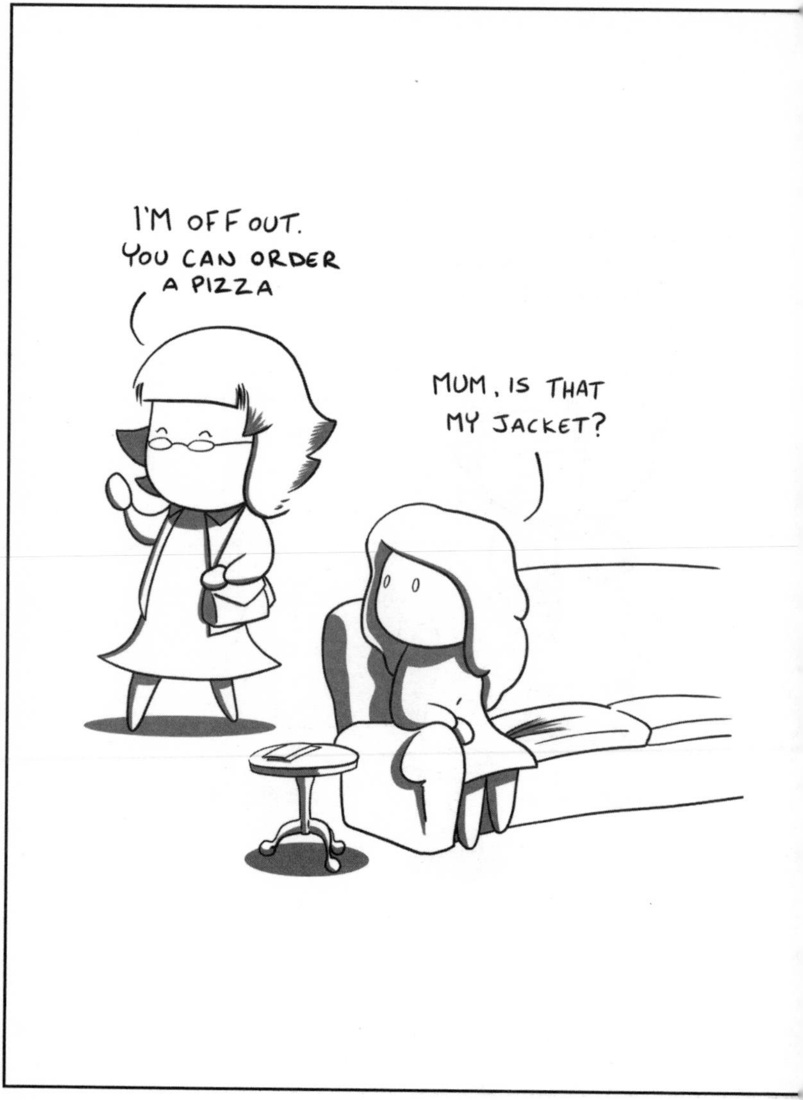
I'M OFF OUT. YOU CAN ORDER A PIZZA
MUM, IS THAT MY JACKET?

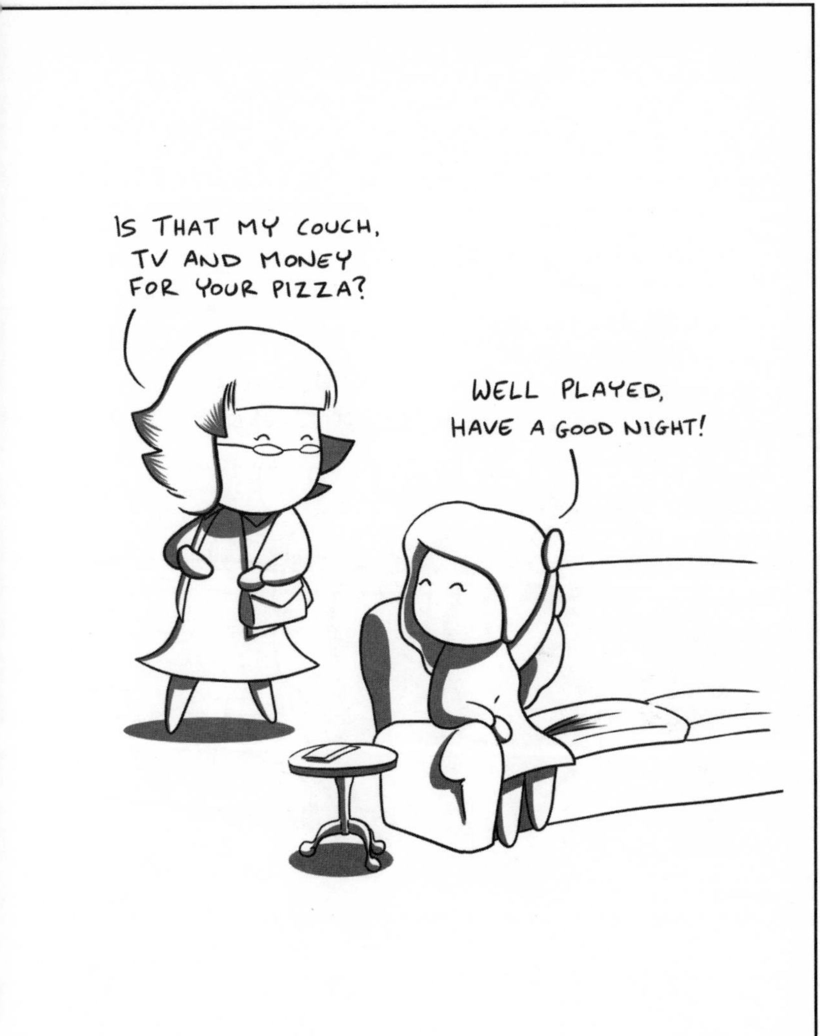
IS THAT MY COUCH, TV AND MONEY FOR YOUR PIZZA?
WELL PLAYED, HAVE A GOOD NIGHT!

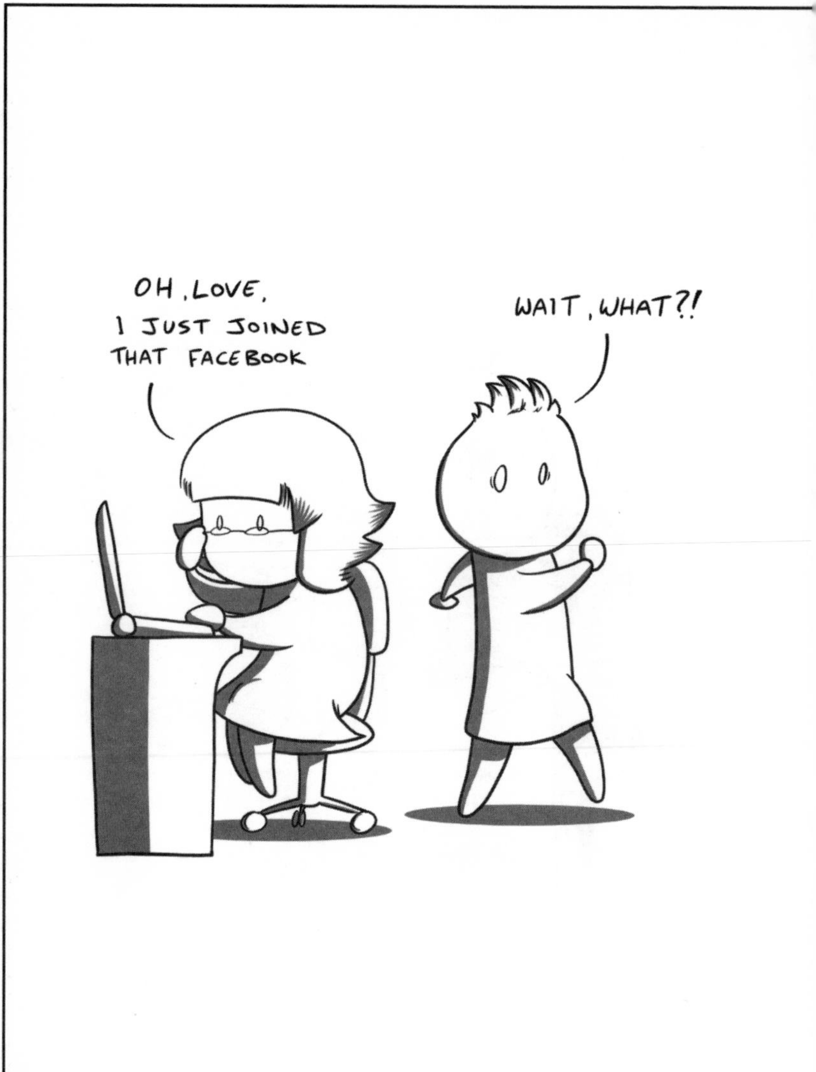
OH, LOVE,
I JUST JOINED
THAT FACEBOOK
WAIT, WHAT?!

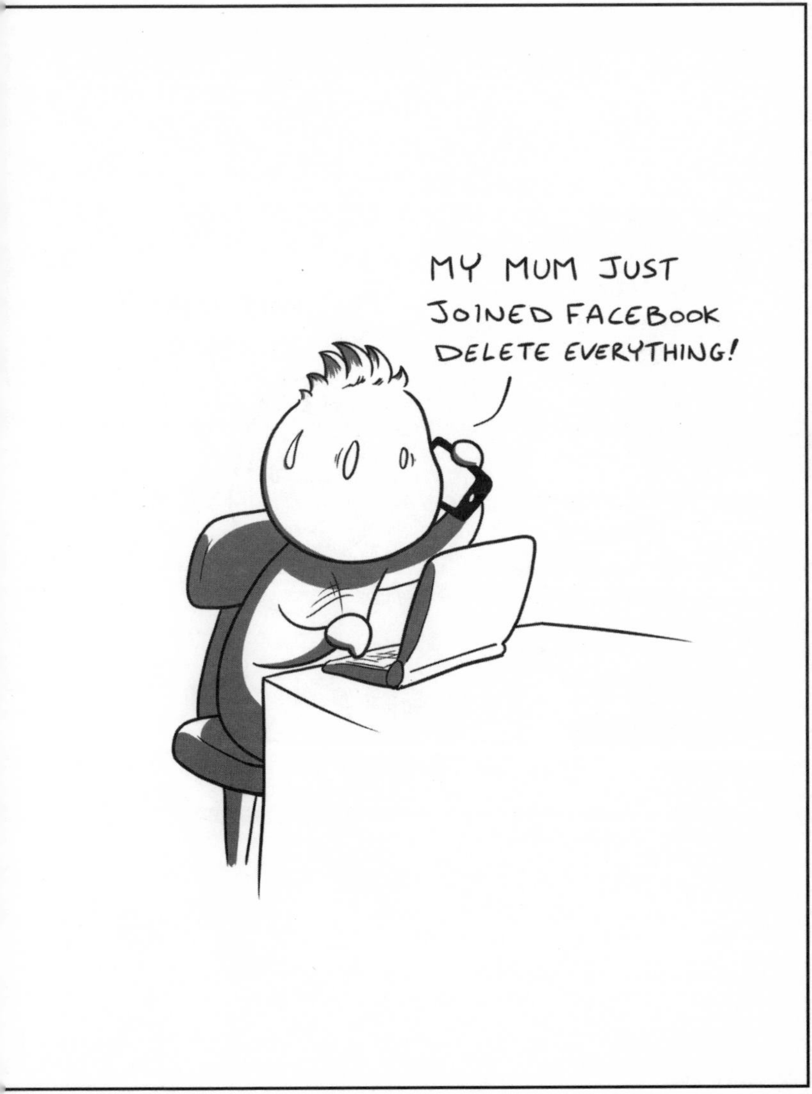
MY MUM JUST JOINED FACEBOOK DELETE EVERYTHING!

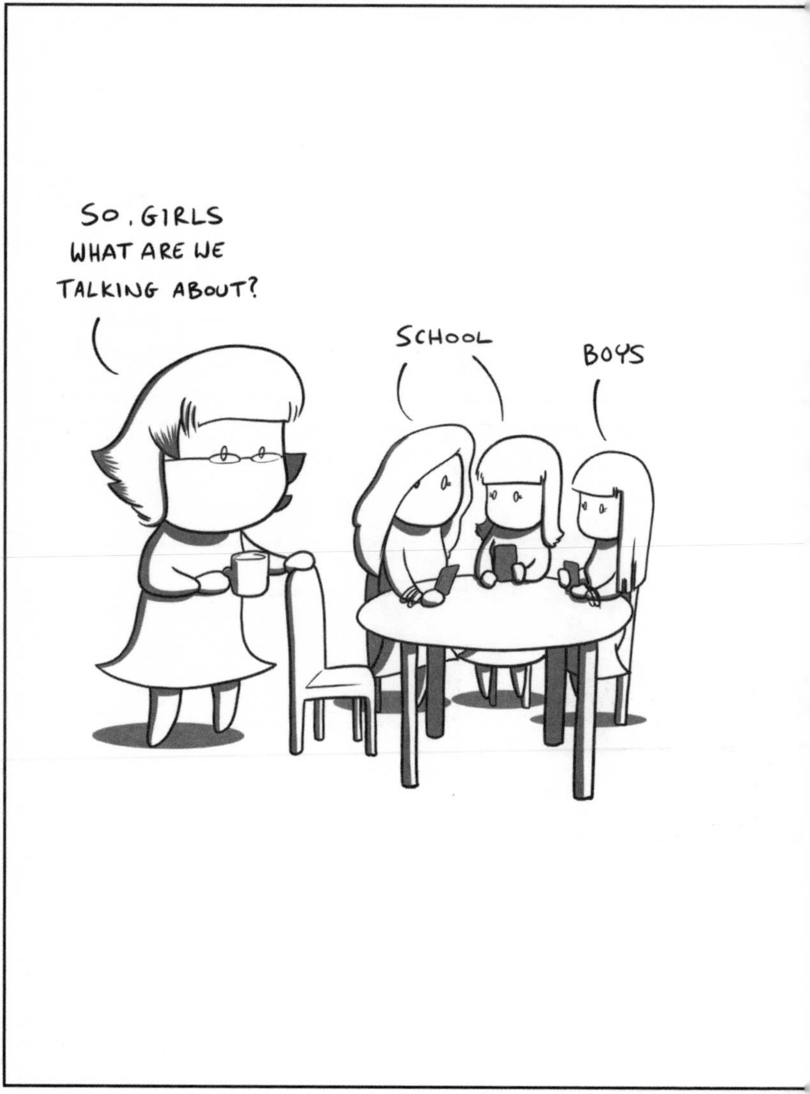
SO, GIRLS WHAT ARE WE TALKING ABOUT?
SCHOOL
BOYS

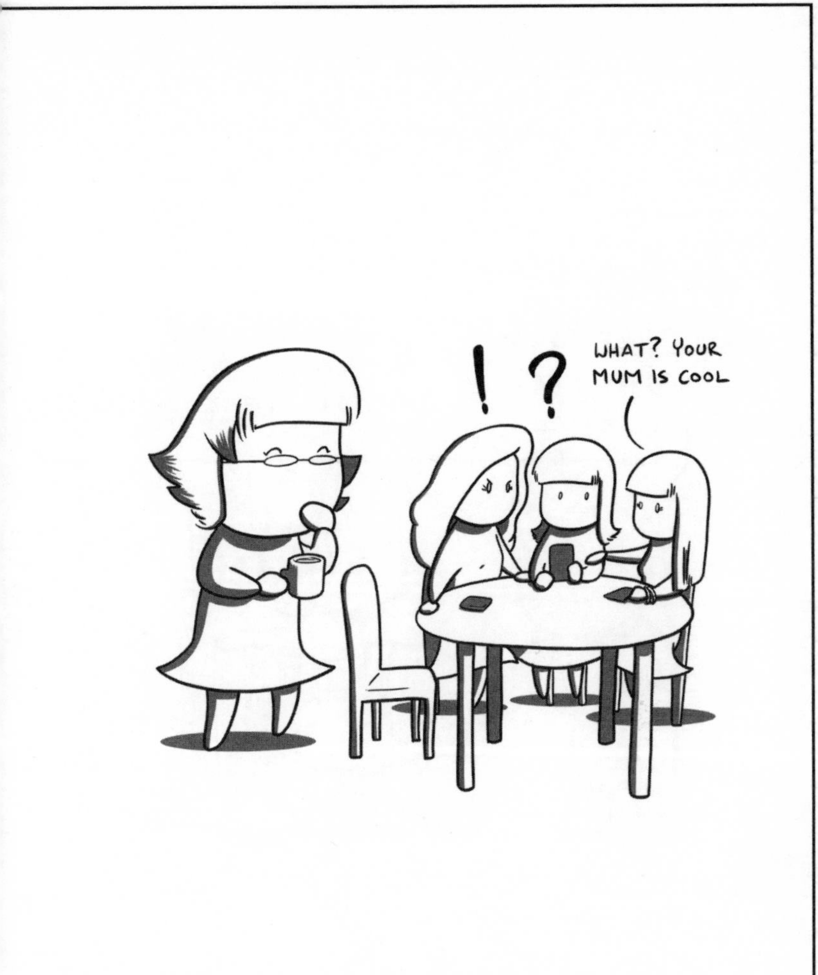
!
?
WHAT? YOUR MUM IS COOL

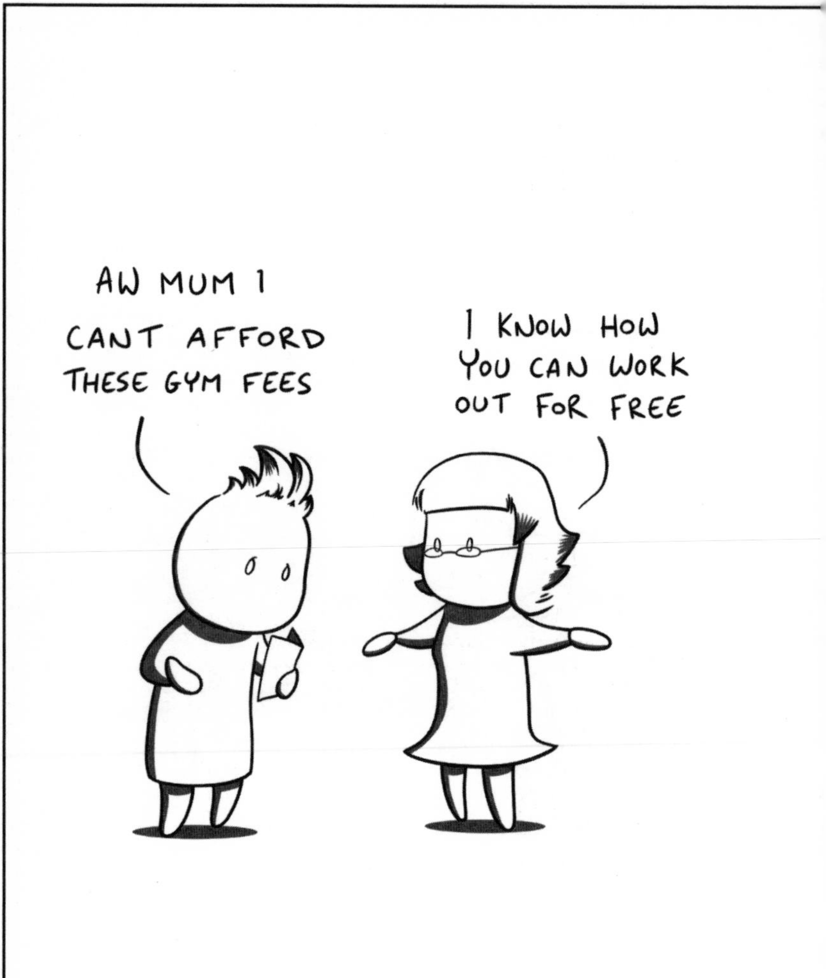
AW MUM I CANT AFFORD THESE GYM FEES
I KNOW HOW YOU CAN WORK OUT FOR FREE

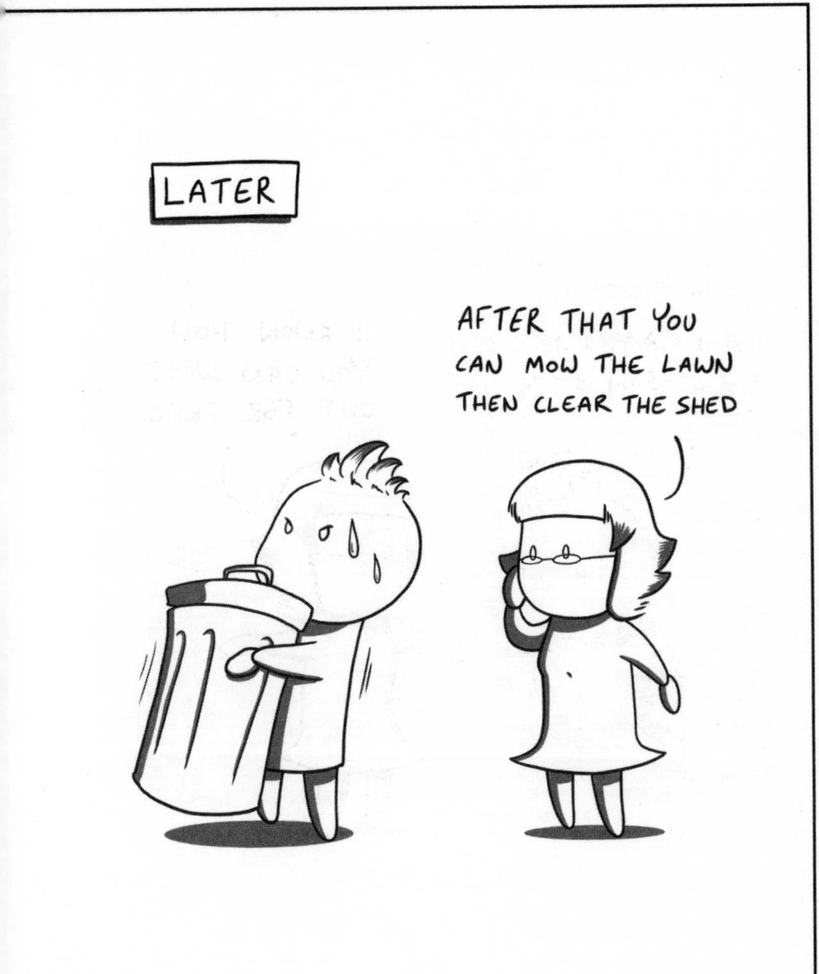
LATER
AFTER THAT YOU CAN MOW THE LAWN THEN CLEAR THE SHED

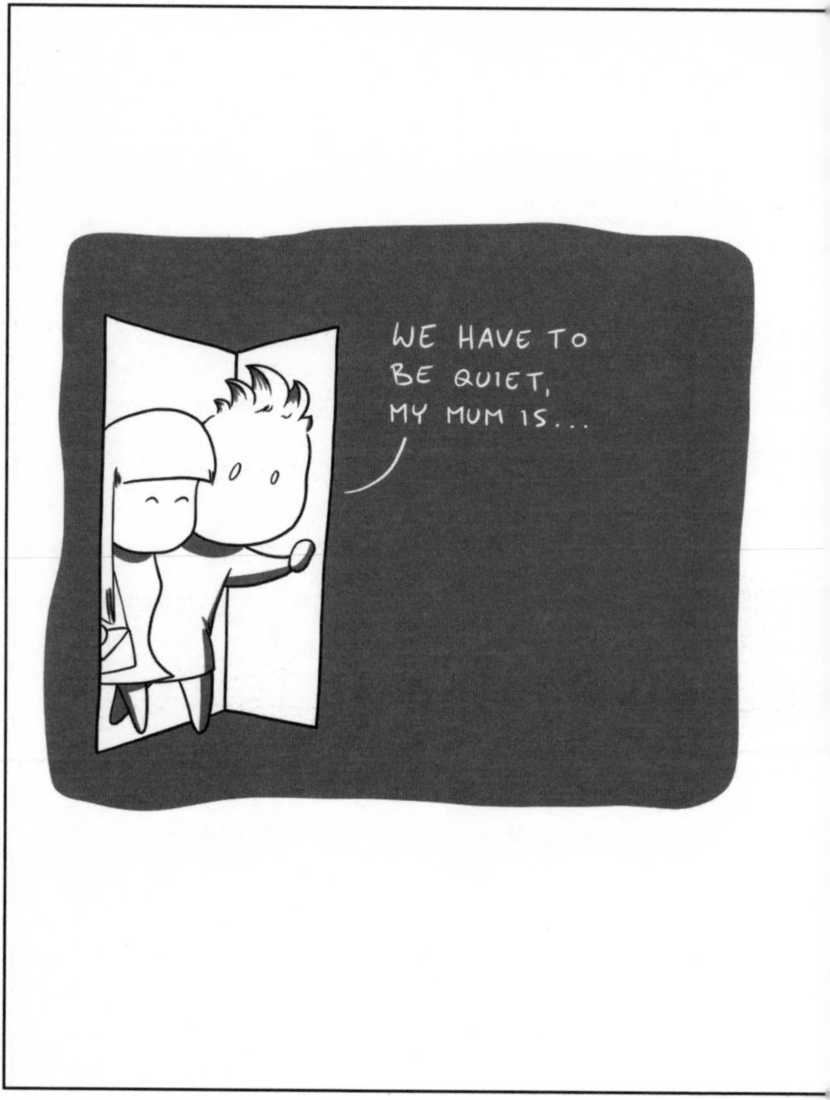
WE HAVE TO BE QUIET, MY MUM IS...

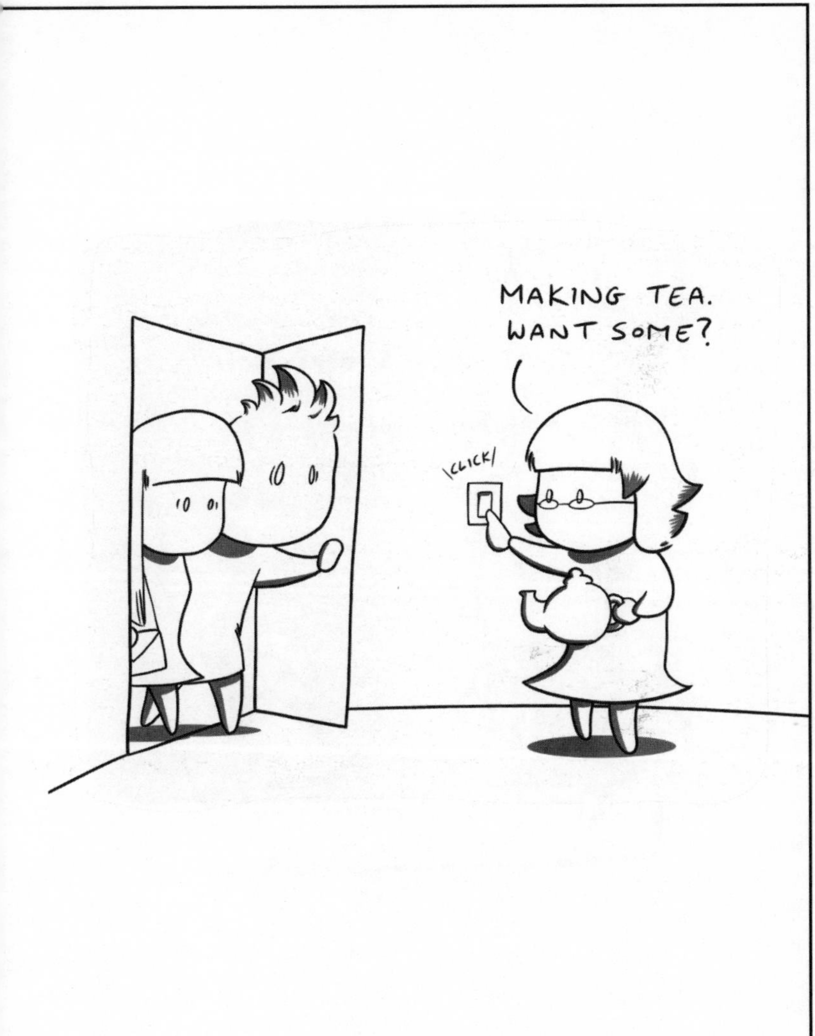
MAKING TEA.
WANT SOME?
\CLICK/

THIS MOVIE IS VERY VIOLENT
WHO'S THAT?
THAT ACTOR'S DEAD NOW
OOH I LOVE HARRISON FORD!
SIGH

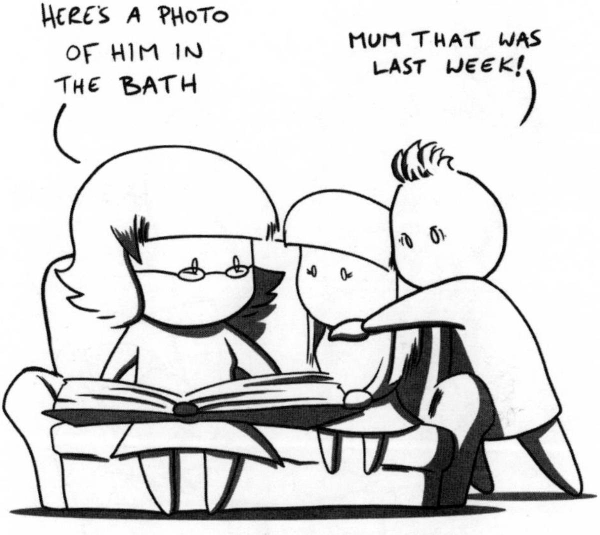
HERE'S A PHOTO OF HIM IN THE BATH
MUM THAT WAS LAST WEEK!

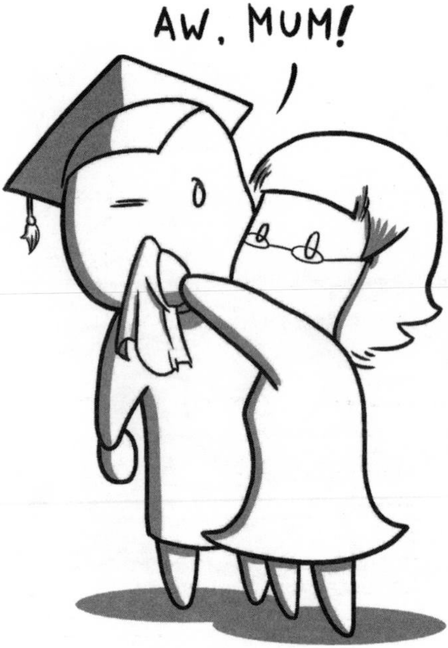
AW, MUM!

 👍 45

MUM
LOOKING GOOD!
TAKE CARE, CALL ME WHEN YOU'RE HOME x

MUM DID YOU POST A PHOTO OF ME IN A HOSPITAL GOWN?!
YOU LOOKED CUTE IN IT

MY MUM
LOVES ME
EVEN
THOUGH...

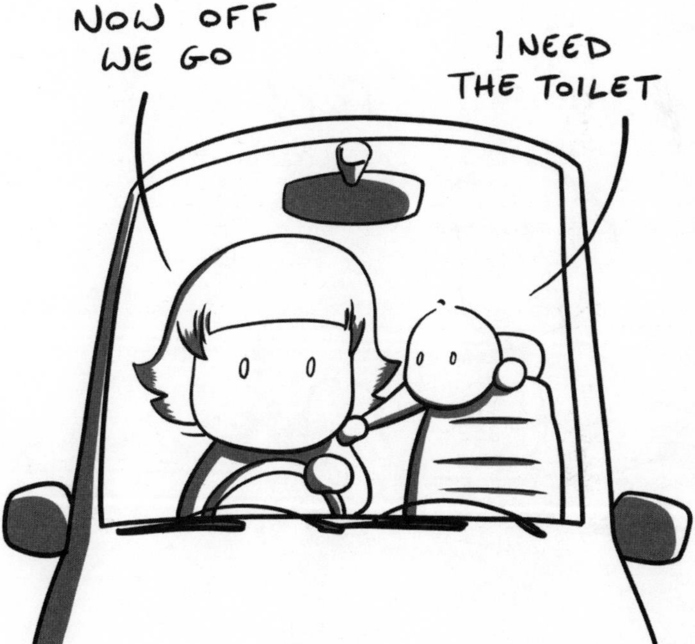
NOW OFF WE GO
I NEED THE TOILET

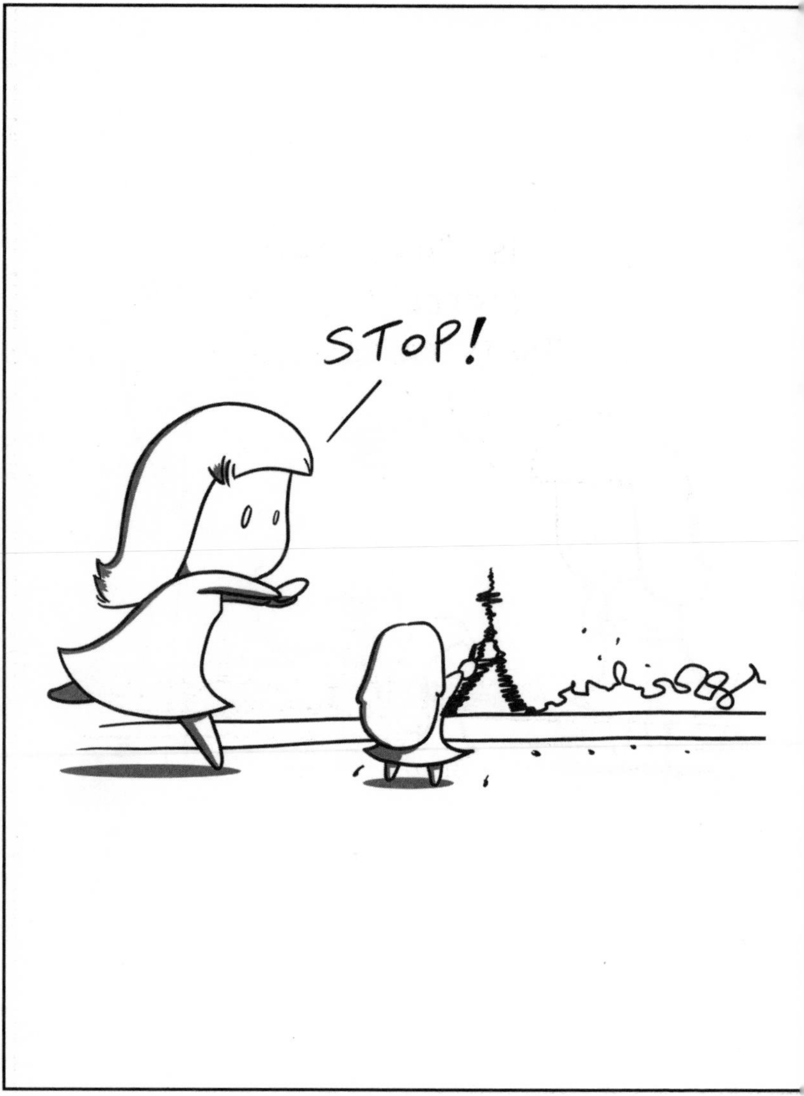
STOP!

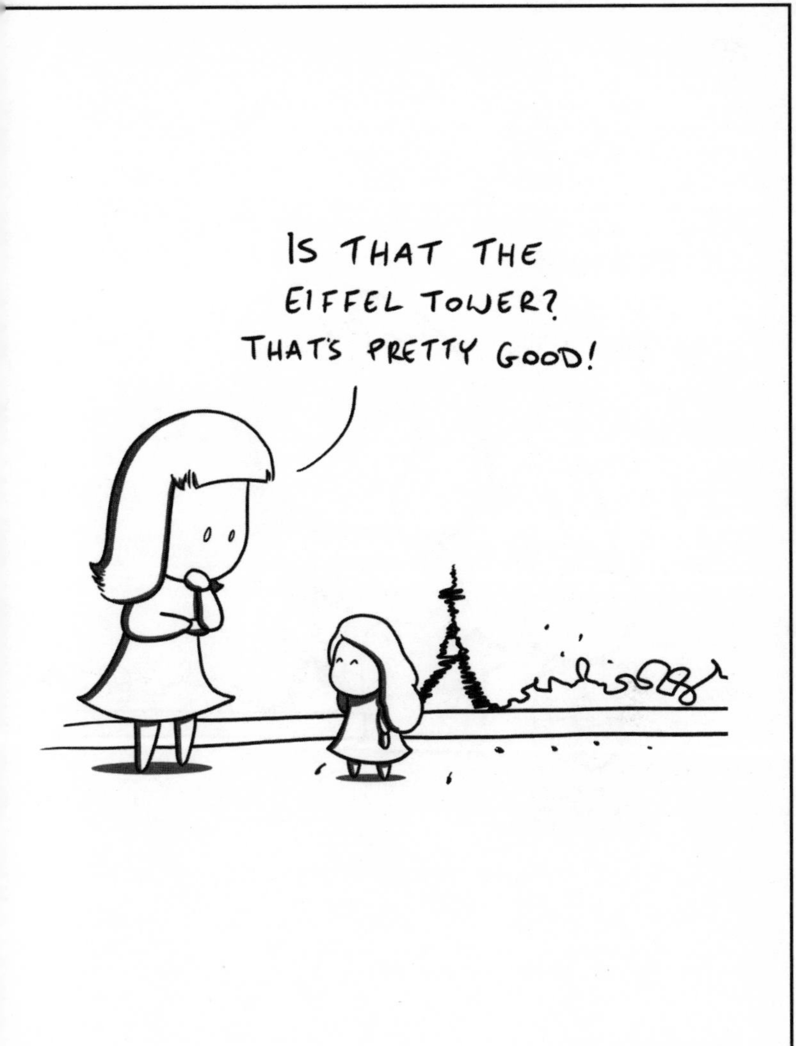
IS THAT THE EIFFEL TOWER? THAT'S PRETTY GOOD!

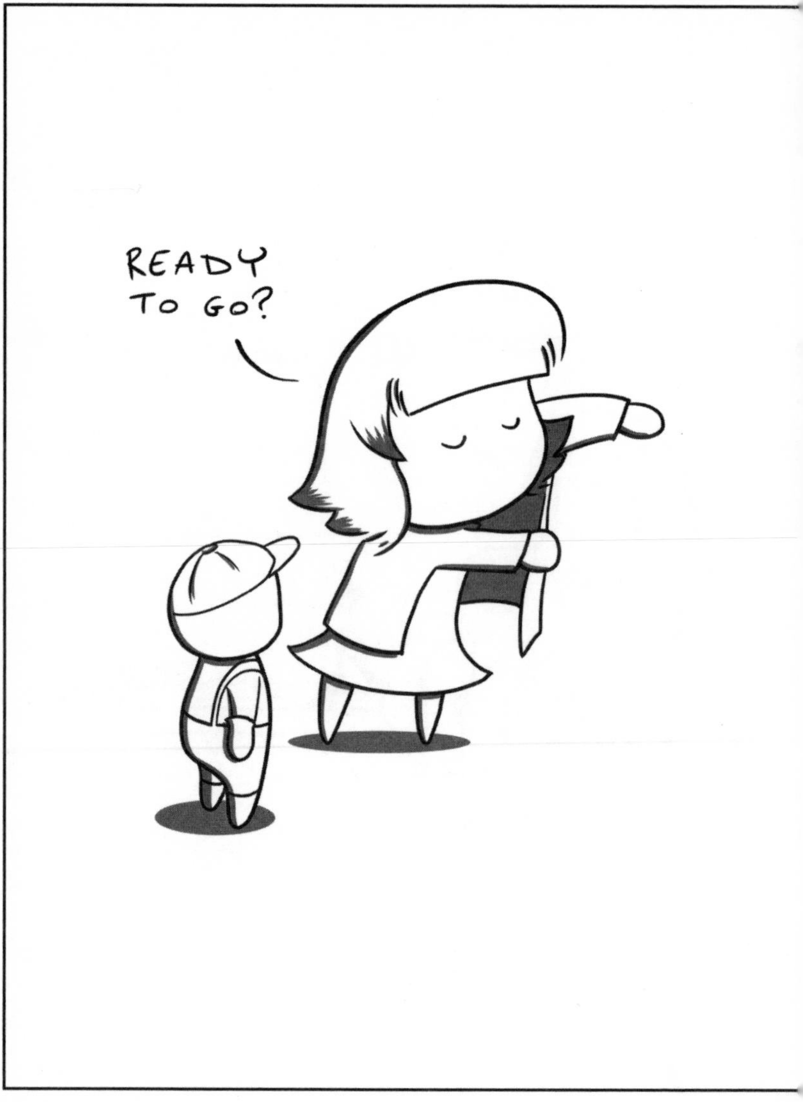
READY
TO GO?

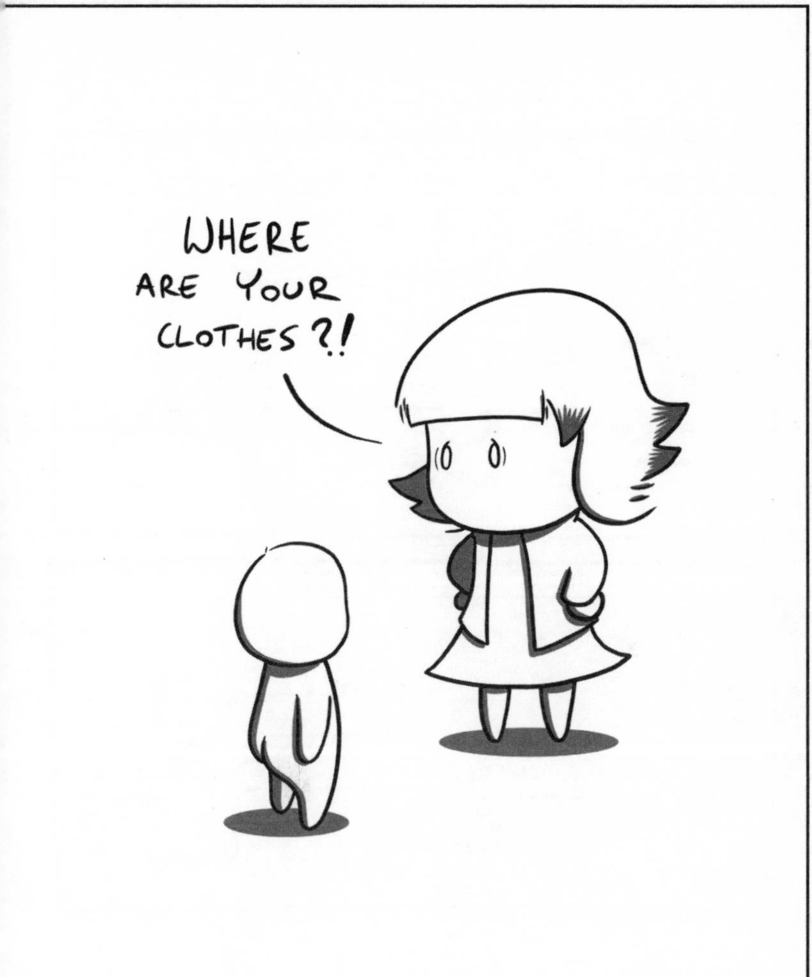
WHERE ARE YOUR CLOTHES?!

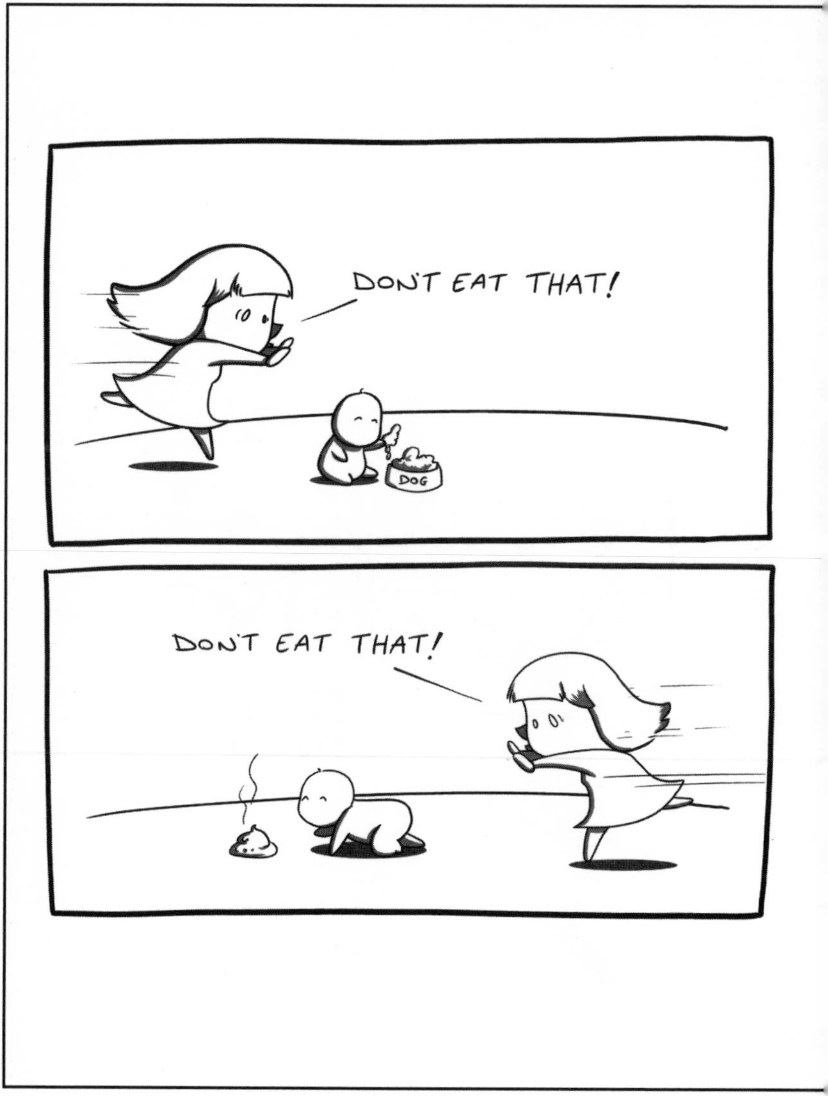
DON'T EAT THAT!
DOG
DON'T EAT THAT!

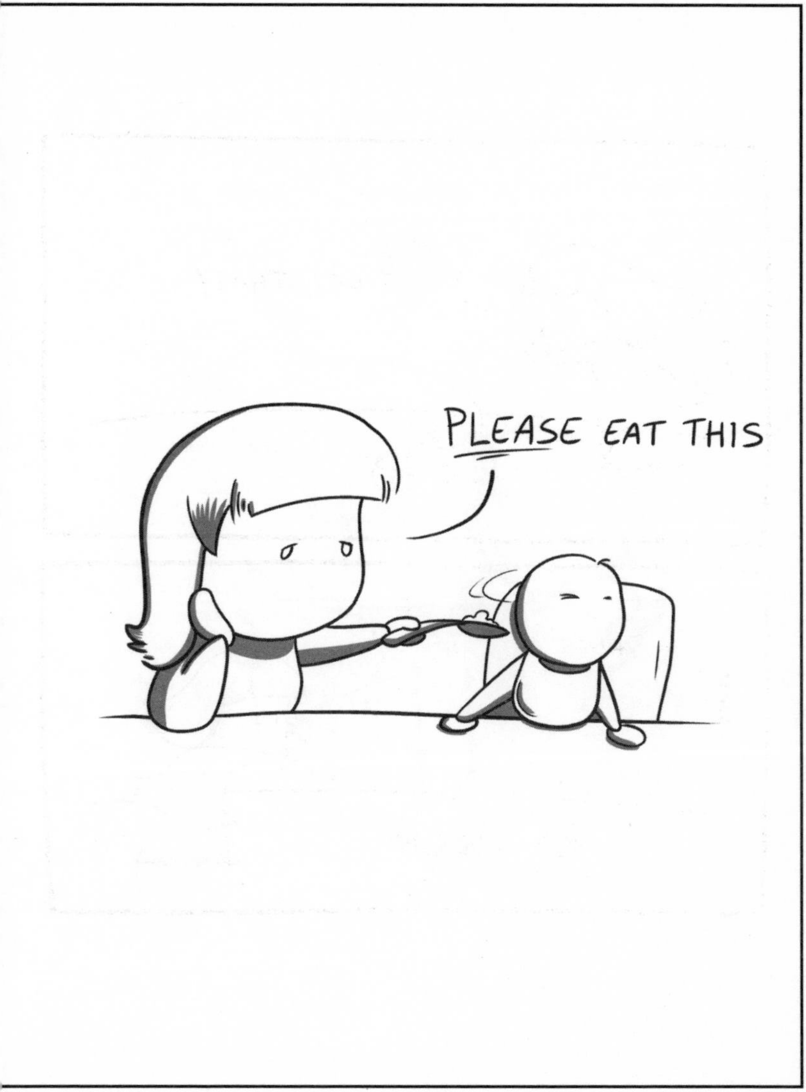
PLEASE EAT THIS

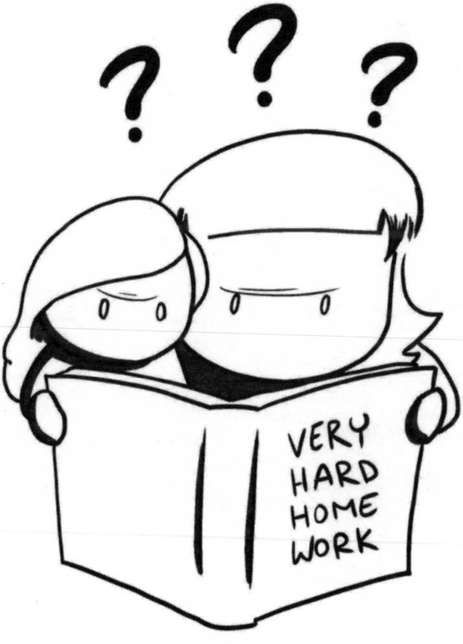
VERY
HARD
HOME
WORK

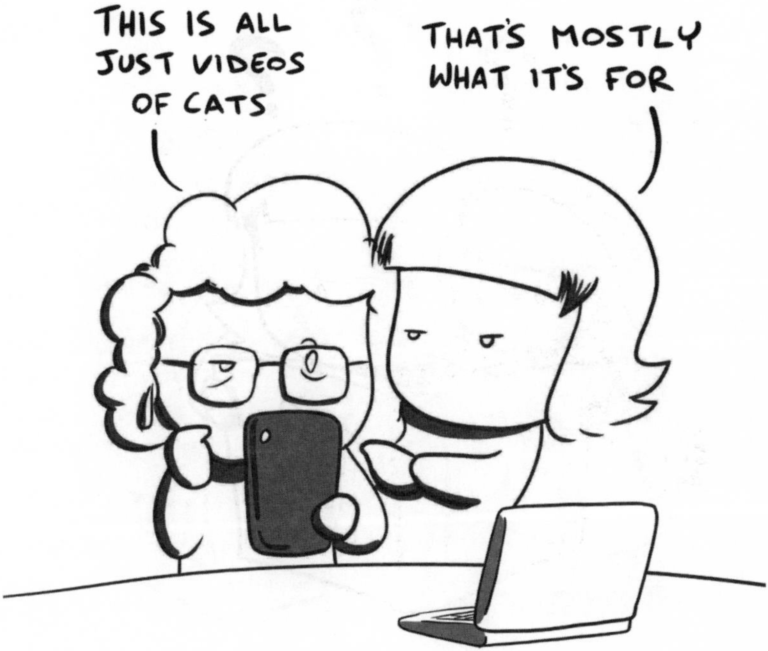
THIS IS ALL JUST VIDEOS OF CATS
THAT'S MOSTLY WHAT IT'S FOR

DO YOU WANT ANYTHING IN THE SHOP?
I NEED A MOTHER'S DAY CARD
THANKS, MUM

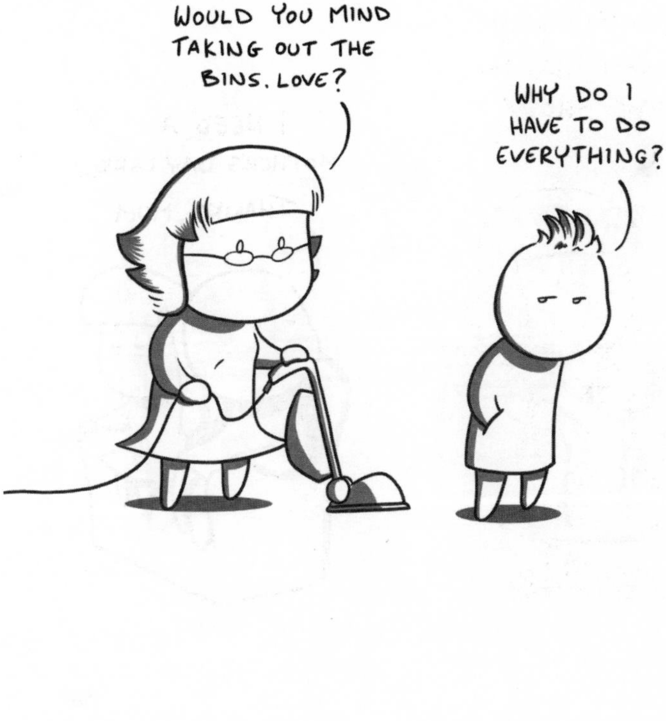
WOULD YOU MIND TAKING OUT THE BINS, LOVE?
WHY DO I HAVE TO DO EVERYTHING?

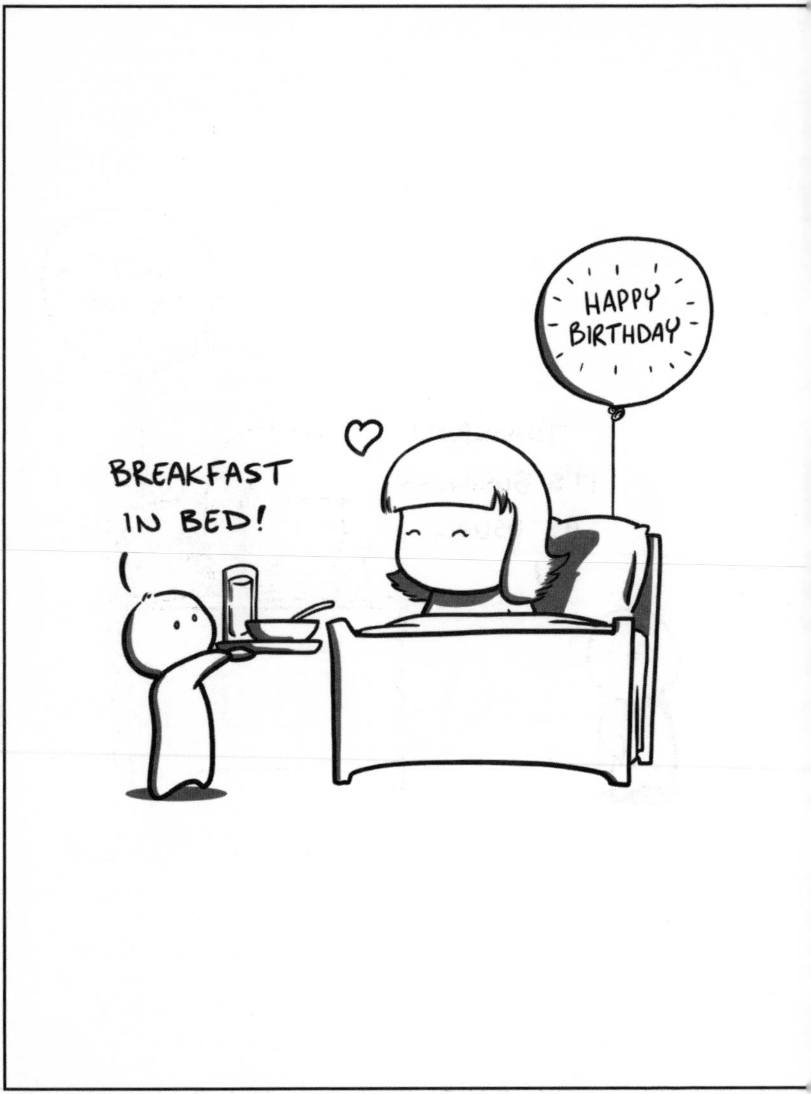
HAPPY BIRTHDAY
BREAKFAST IN BED!

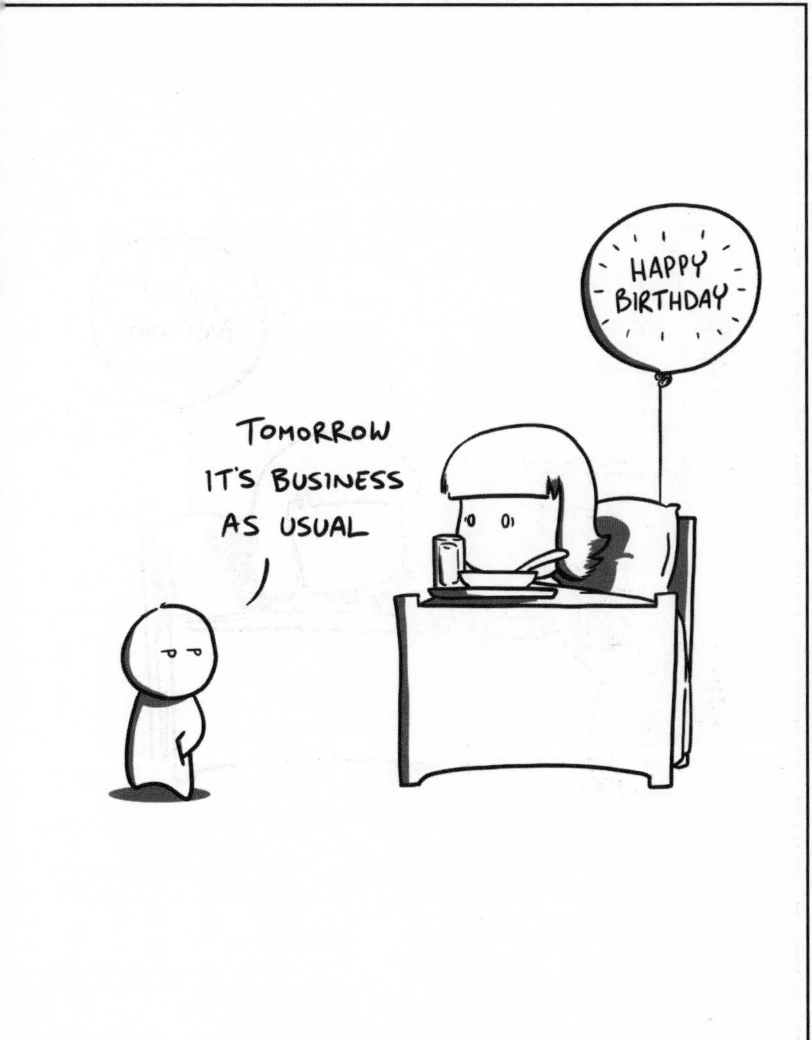
HAPPY BIRTHDAY
TOMORROW IT'S BUSINESS AS USUAL

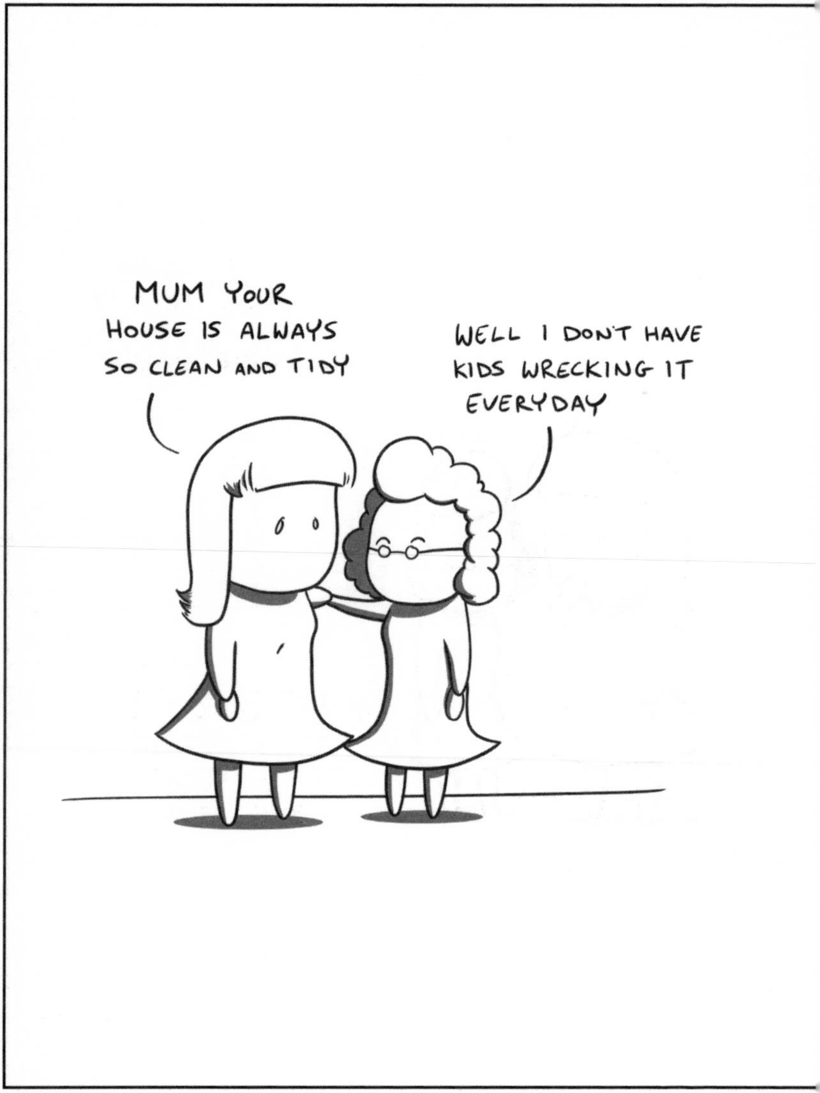
MUM YOUR HOUSE IS ALWAYS SO CLEAN AND TIDY
WELL I DON'T HAVE KIDS WRECKING IT EVERYDAY

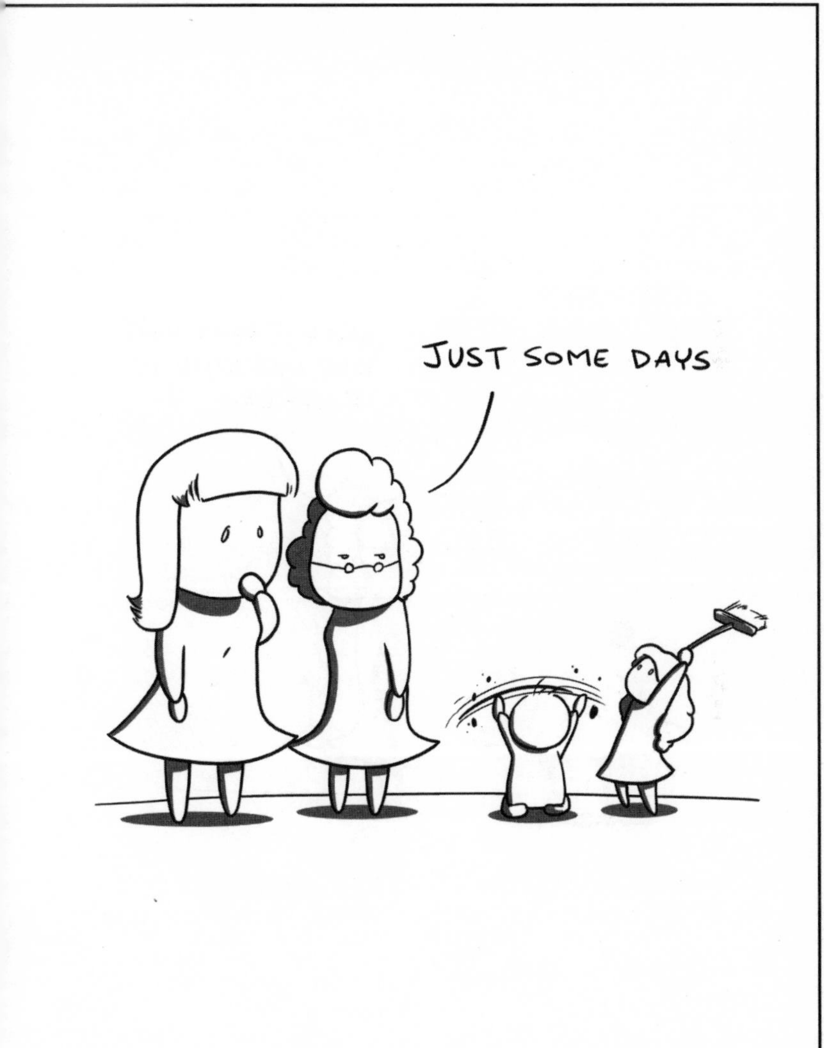
JUST SOME DAYS

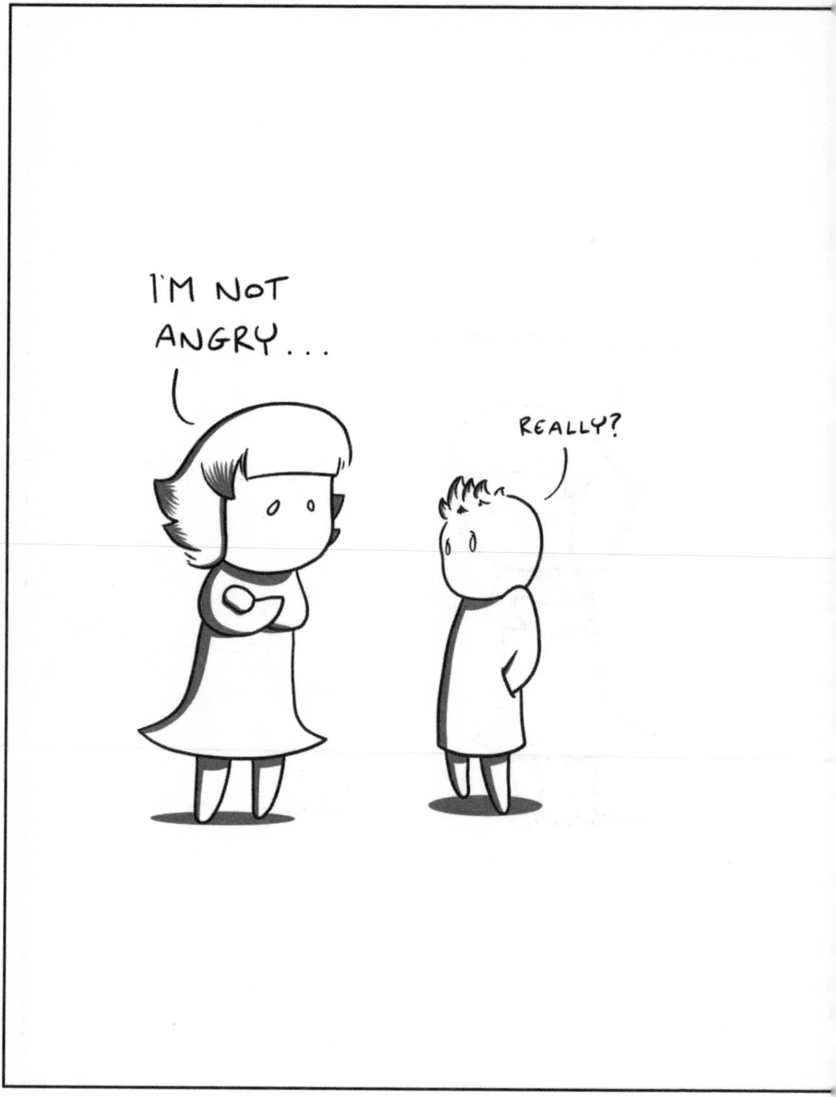
I'M NOT ANGRY...
REALLY?

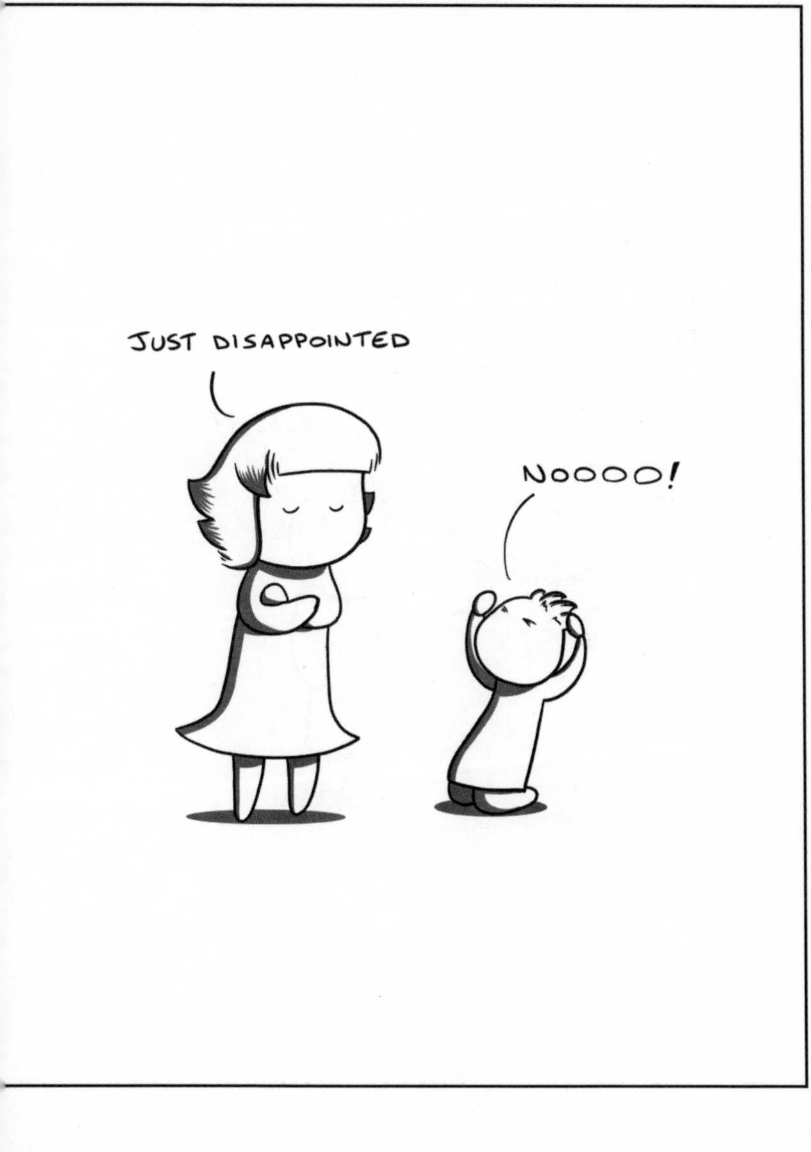
JUST DISAPPOINTED
NOOOO!

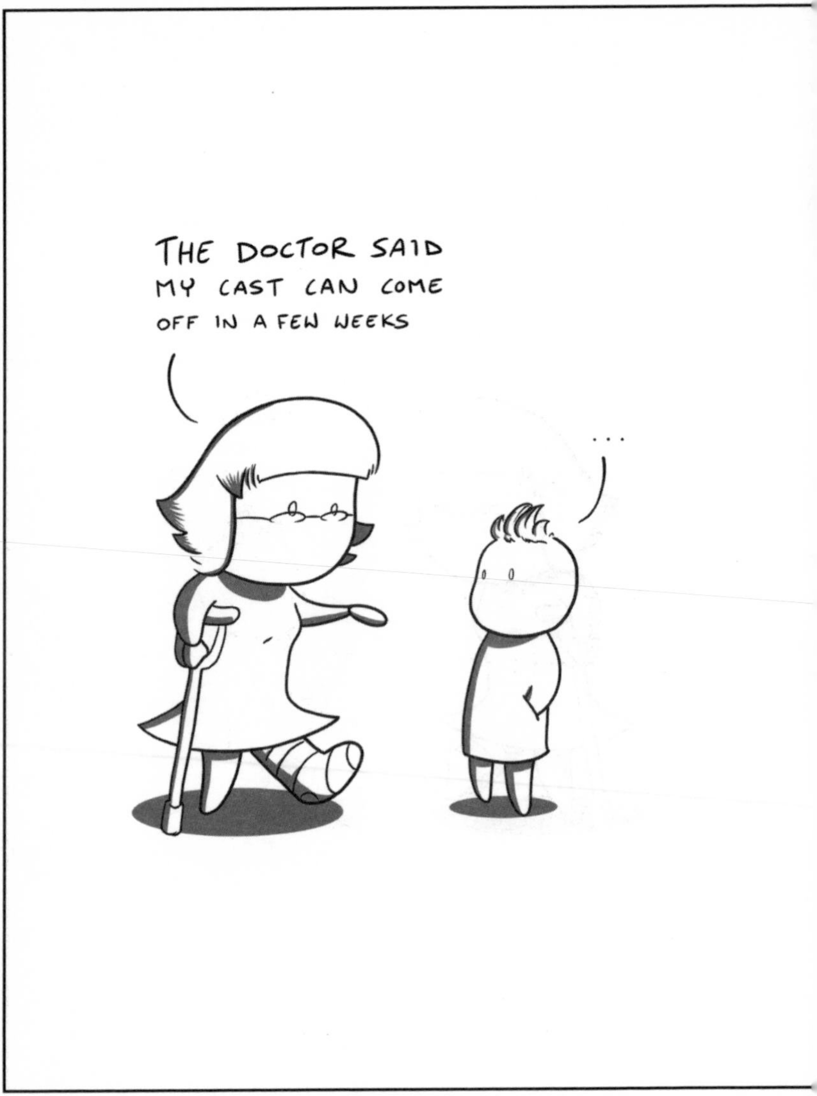
THE DOCTOR SAID MY CAST CAN COME OFF IN A FEW WEEKS
...

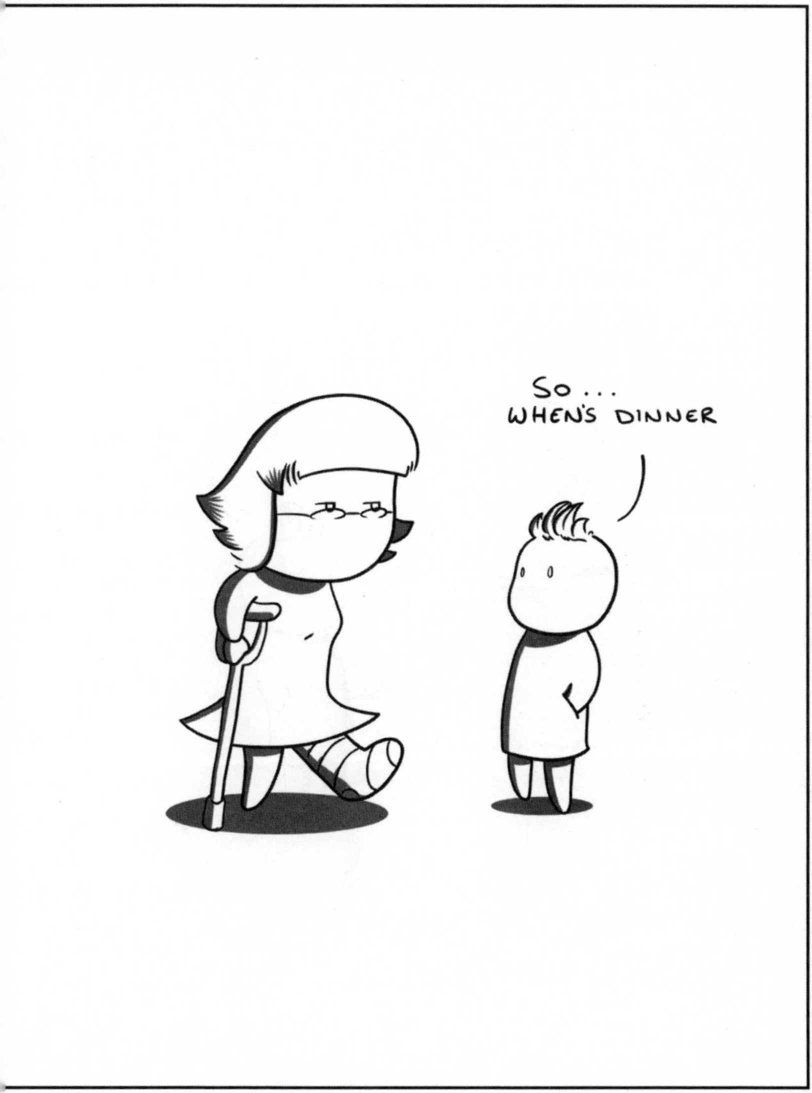
SO ...
WHEN'S DINNER

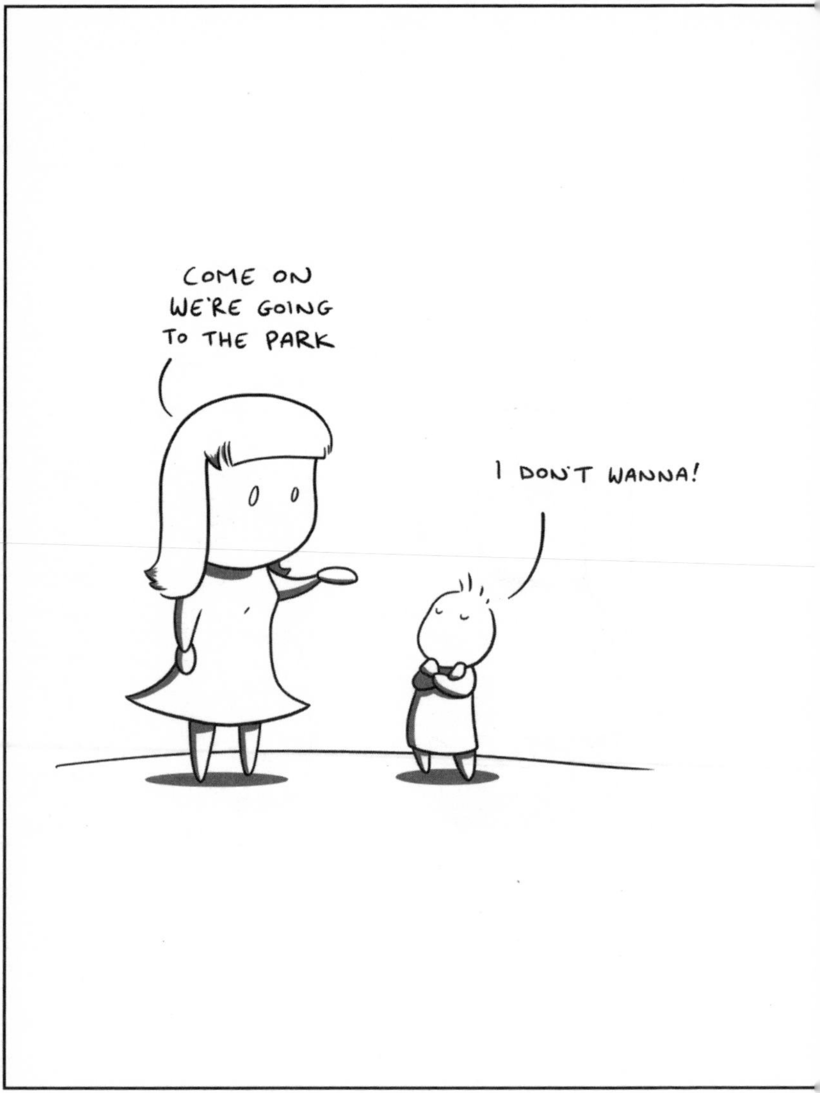
COME ON WE'RE GOING TO THE PARK
I DON'T WANNA!

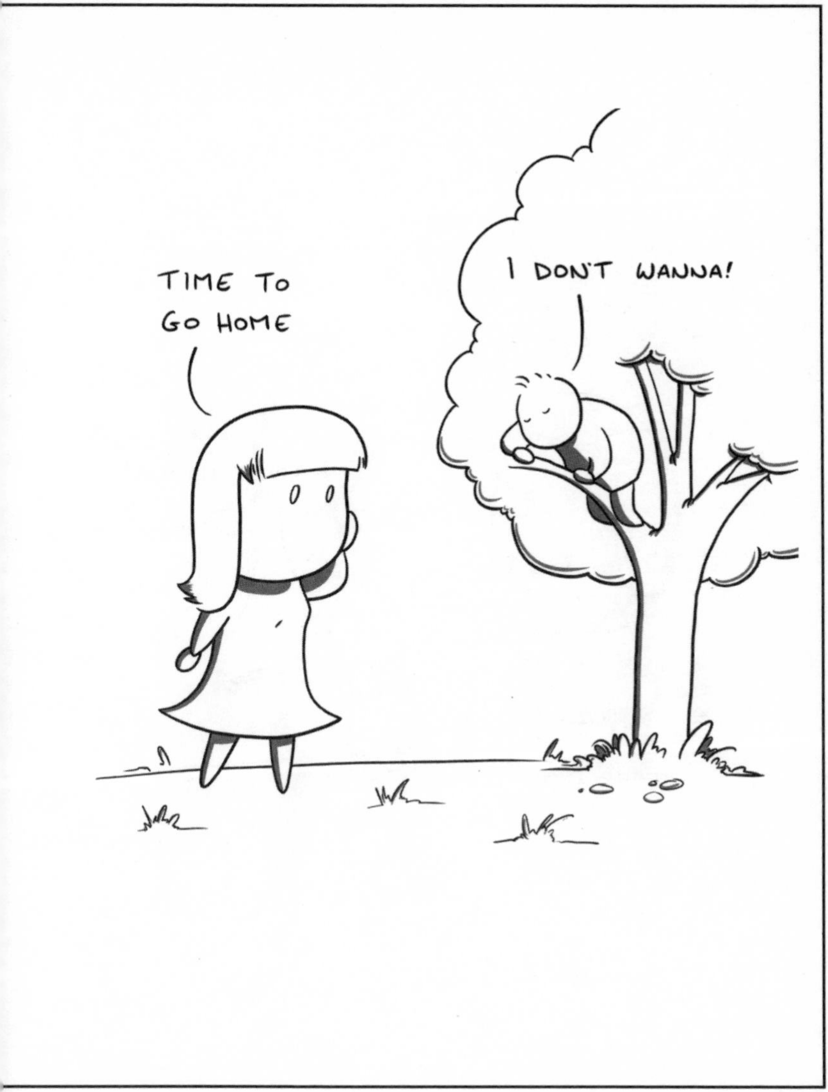
TIME TO
GO HOME
I DON'T WANNA!

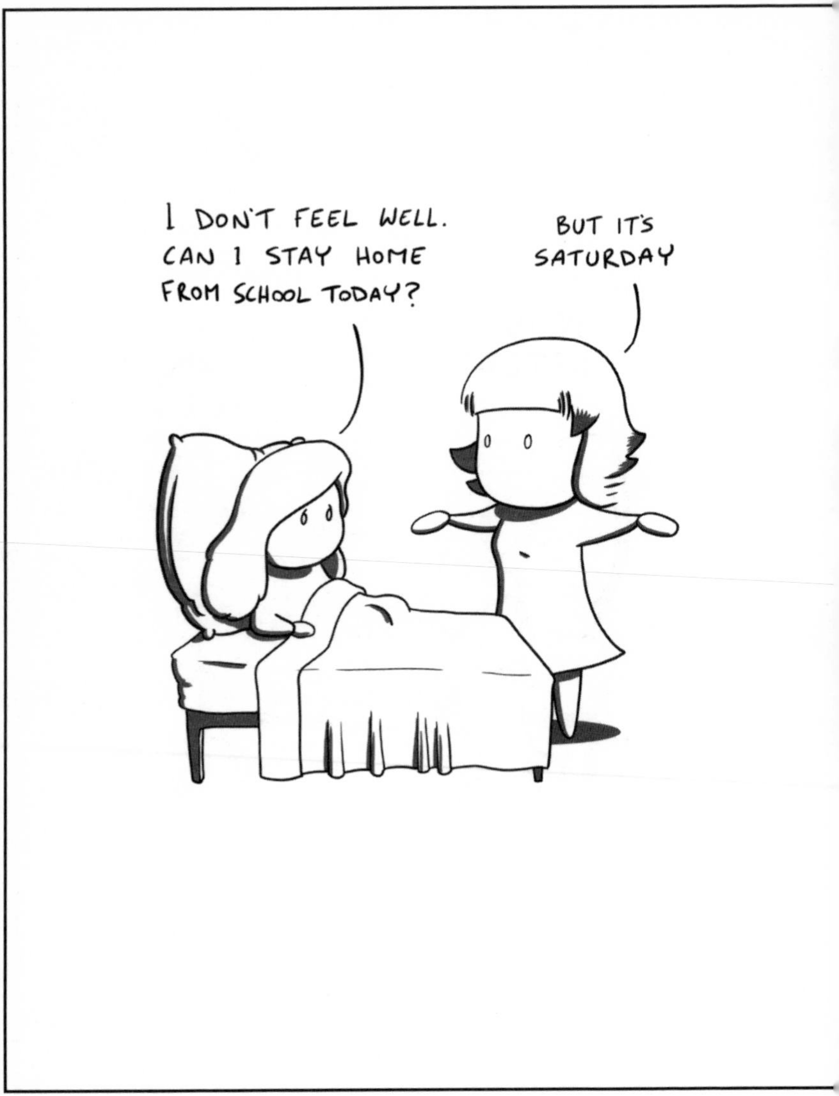
I DON'T FEEL WELL. CAN I STAY HOME FROM SCHOOL TODAY?
BUT IT'S SATURDAY

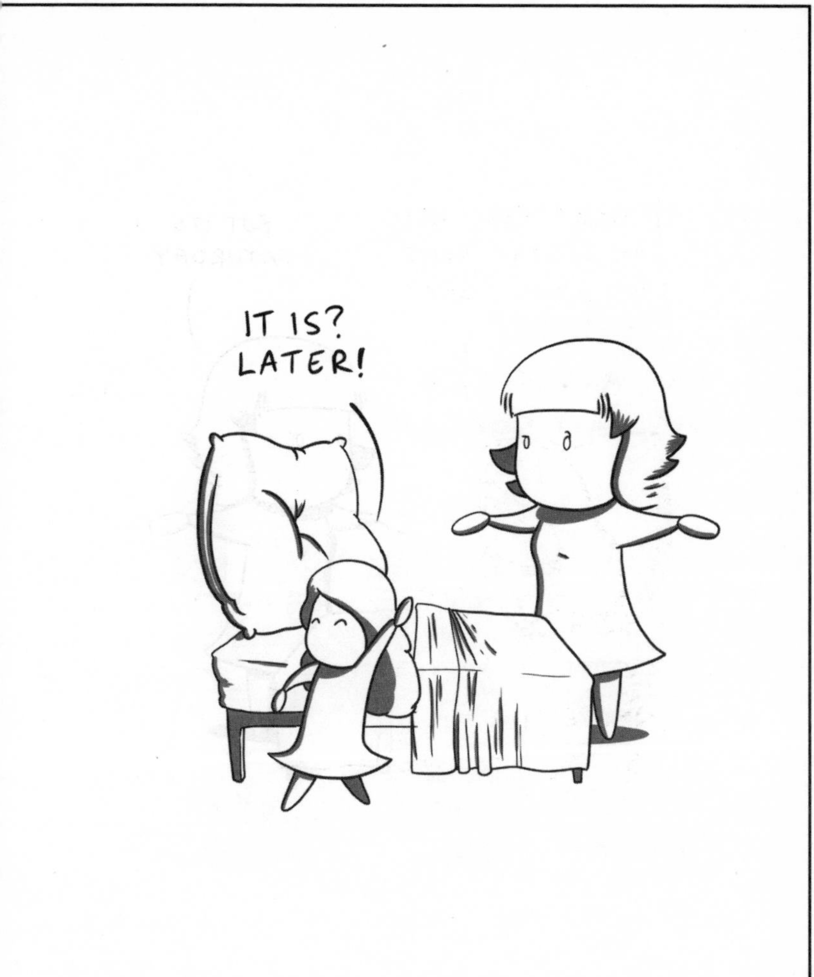
IT IS? LATER!

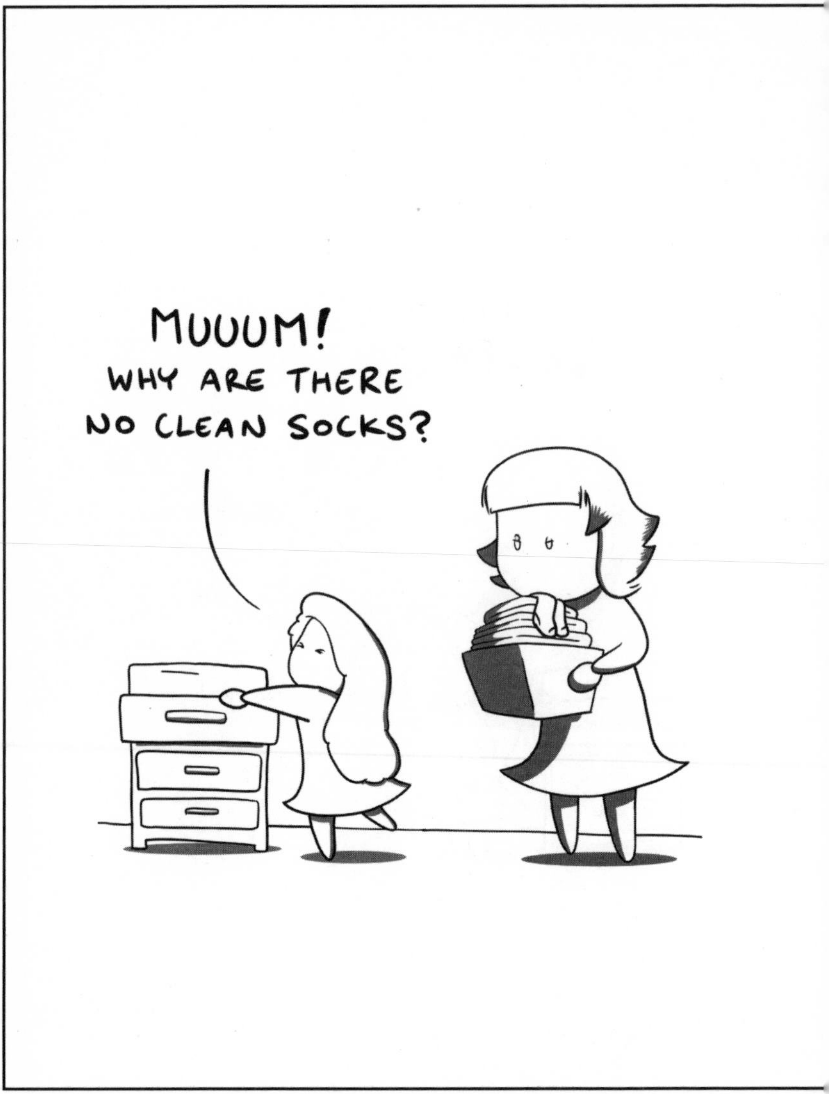
MUUUM!
WHY ARE THERE
NO CLEAN SOCKS?

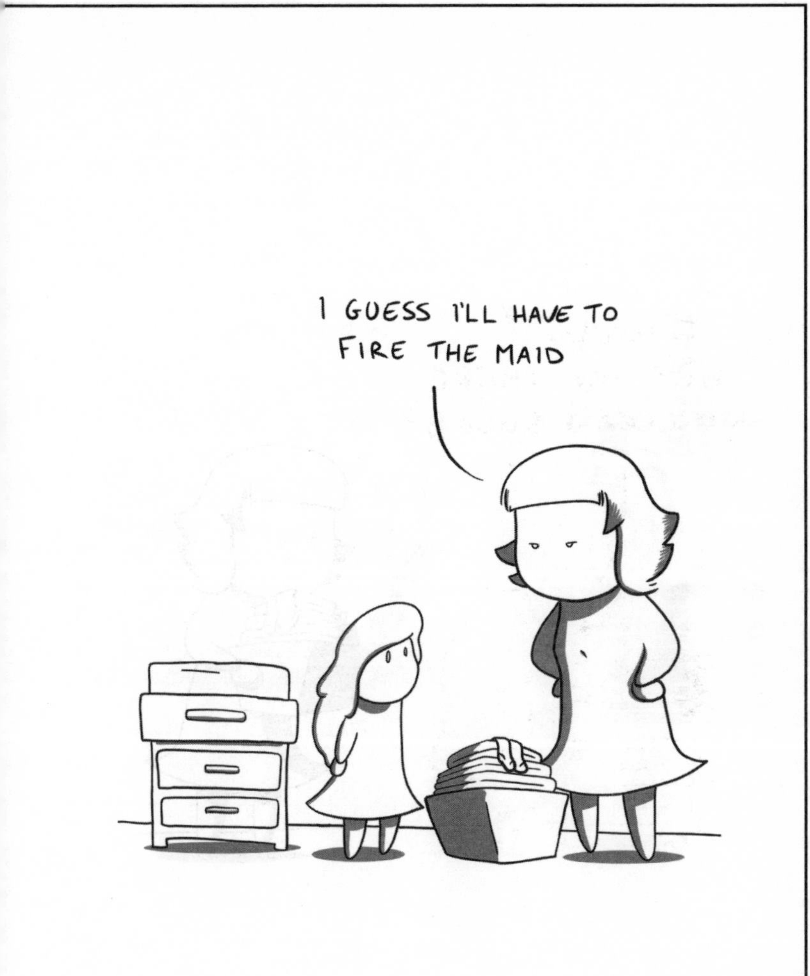
I GUESS I'LL HAVE TO FIRE THE MAID

I'M FINISHED
I GUESS THAT MAKES TWO OF US

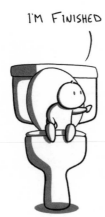

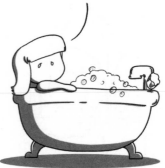

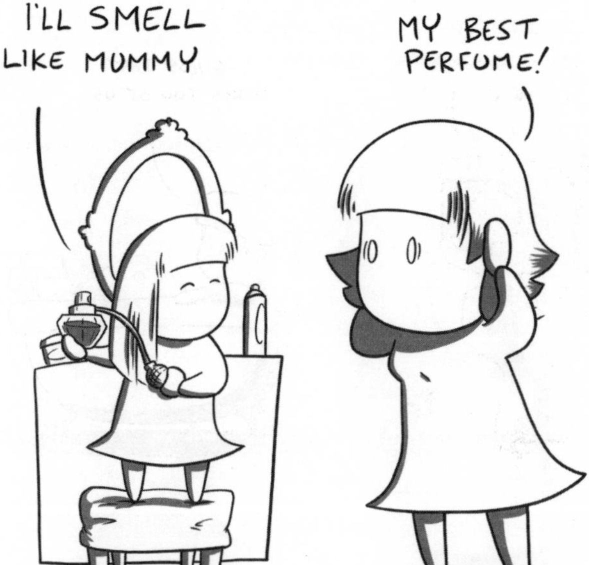
I'LL SMELL LIKE MUMMY
MY BEST PERFUME!

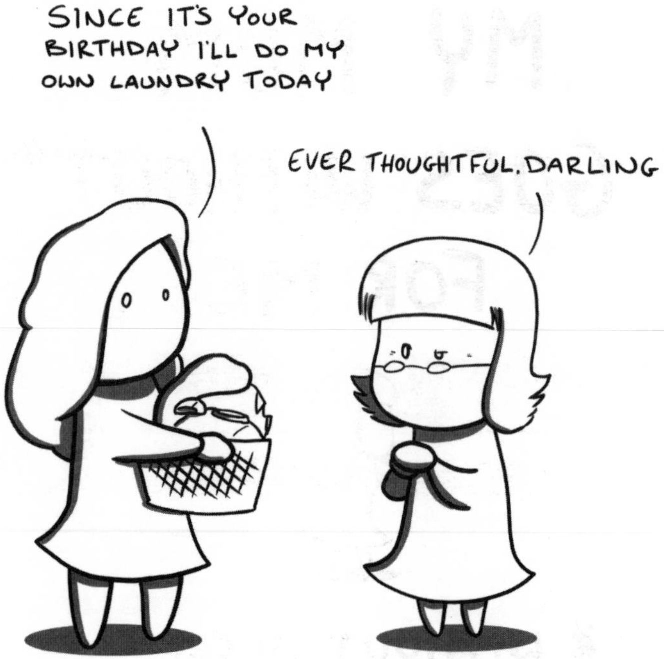
SINCE IT'S YOUR BIRTHDAY I'LL DO MY OWN LAUNDRY TODAY
EVER THOUGHTFUL, DARLING

MY MUM GOES WITHOUT* FOR ME

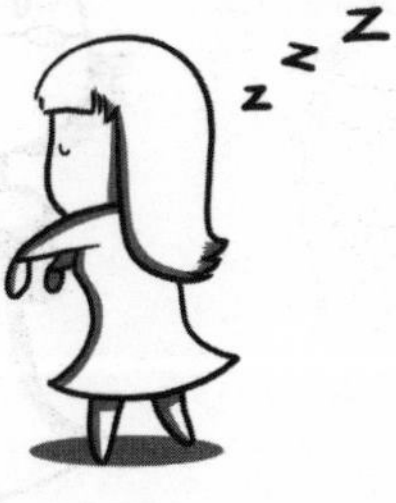
z z z

* WITHOUT SLEEP

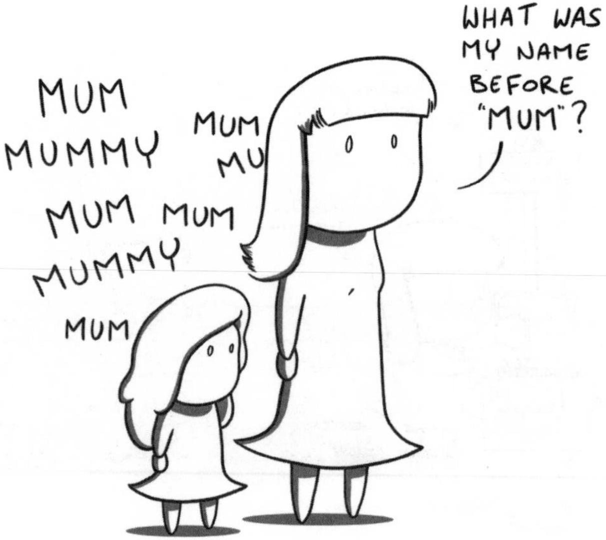
MUM
MUMMY
MUM
MU
MUM MUM
MUMMY
MUM
WHAT WAS MY NAME BEFORE "MUM"?

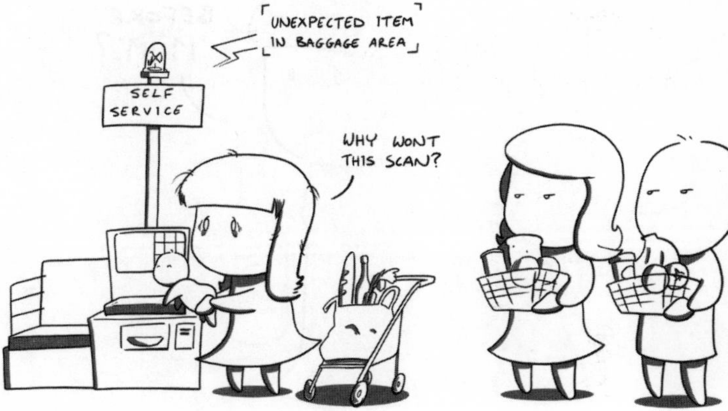
UNEXPECTED ITEM IN BAGGAGE AREA
SELF SERVICE
WHY WONT THIS SCAN?

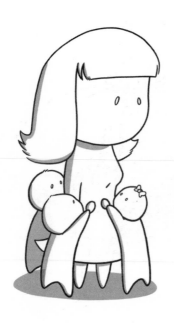

SOON THEY WILL SLEEP AND YOU AND I CAN BE TOGETHER

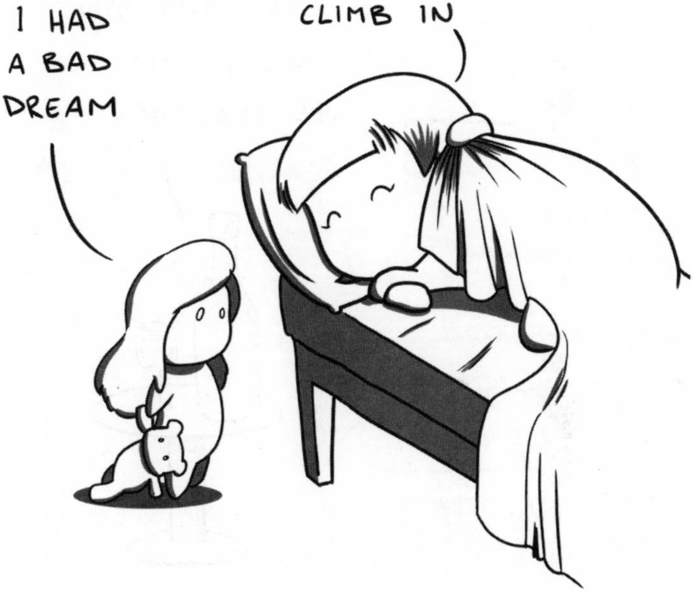
I HAD A BAD DREAM
CLIMB IN

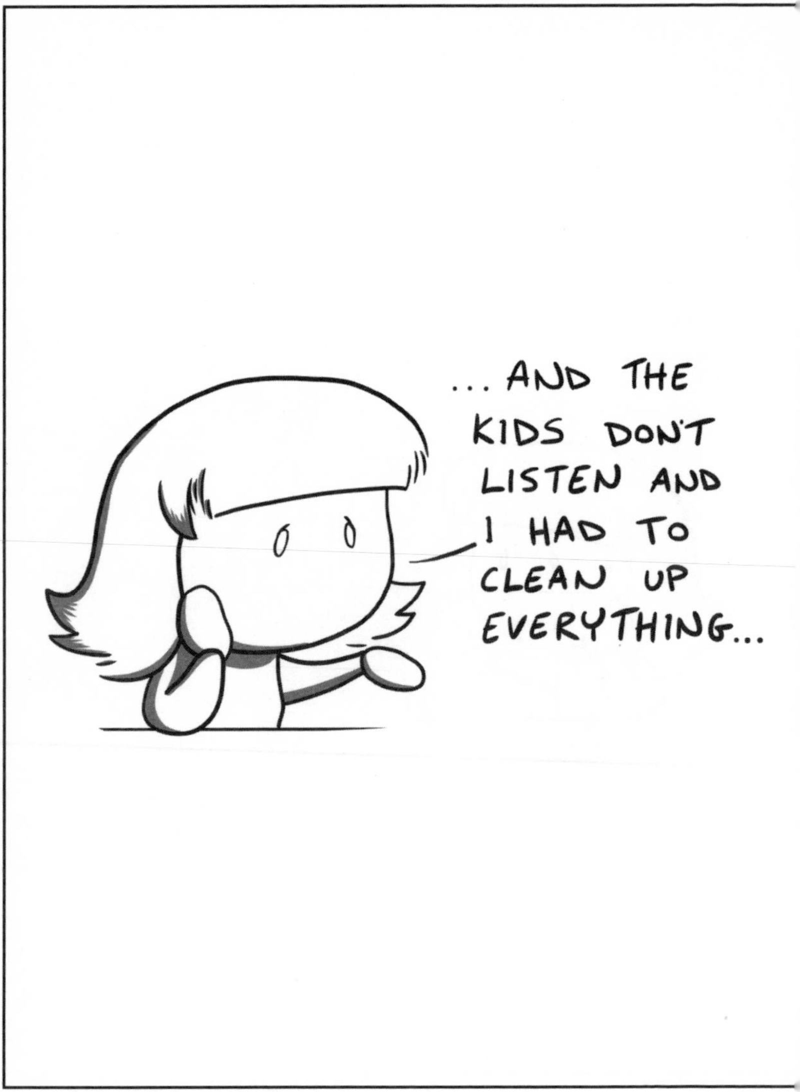
...AND THE KIDS DON'T LISTEN AND I HAD TO CLEAN UP EVERYTHING...

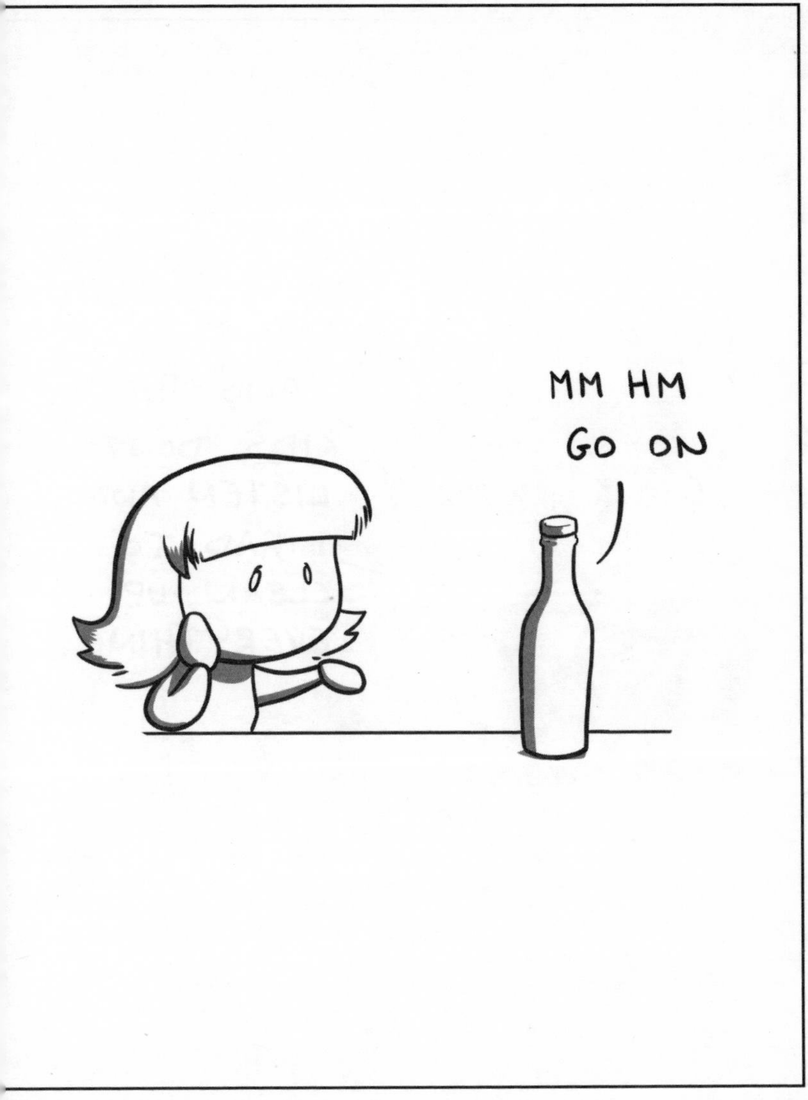
MM HM
GO ON

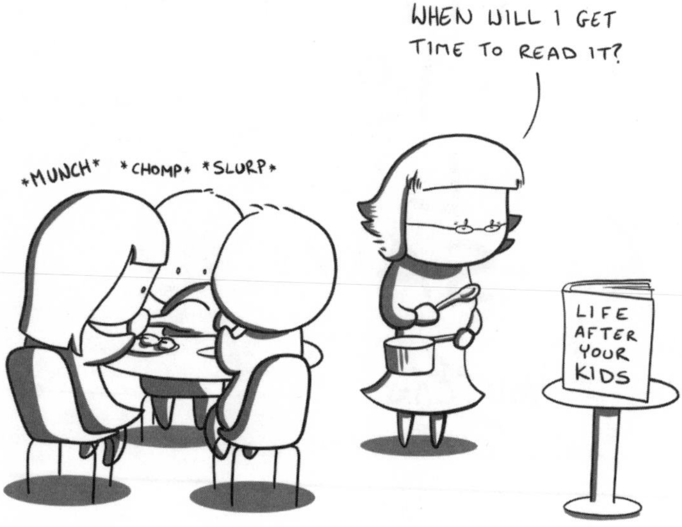
WHEN WILL I GET TIME TO READ IT?
MUNCH *CHOMP* *SLURP*
LIFE AFTER YOUR KIDS

MY MUM IS A LIFE SAVER

YOU CANT SPELL "HERO" WITHOUT HER

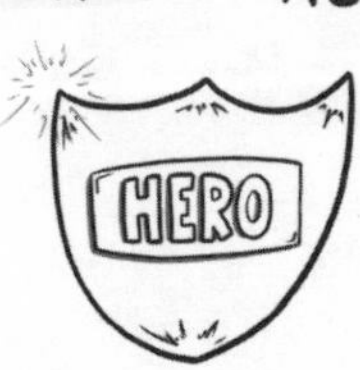
HERO

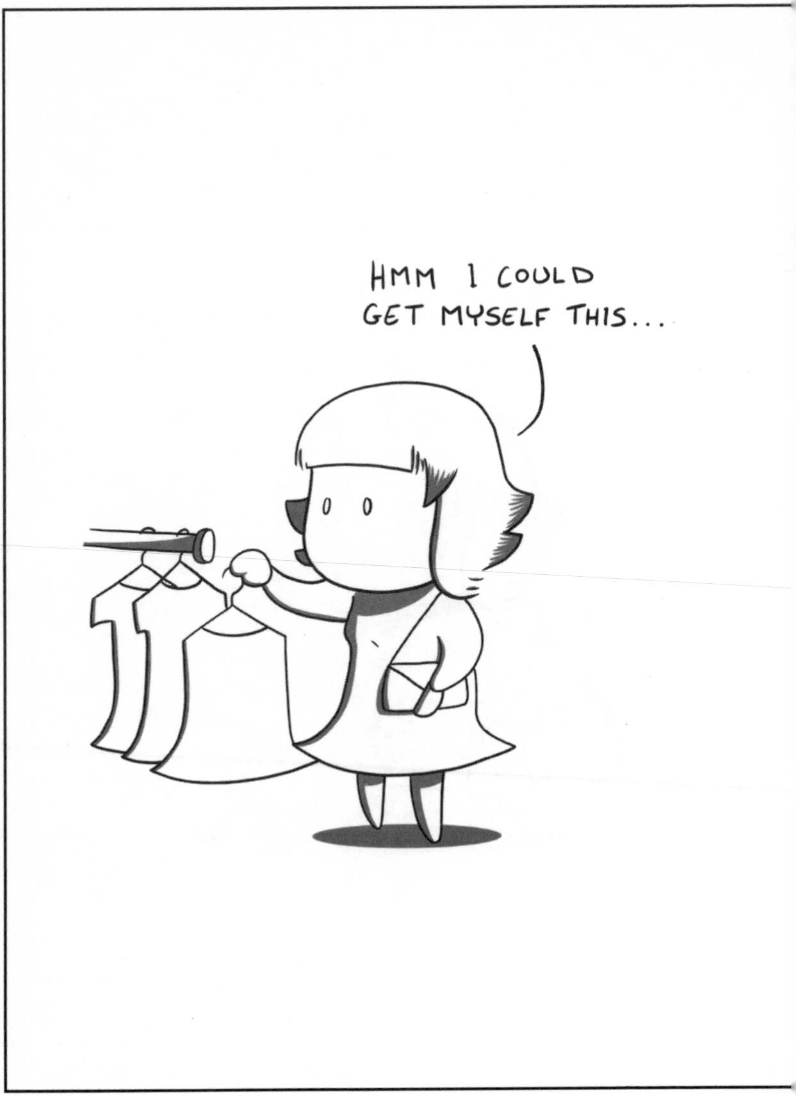
HMM I COULD GET MYSELF THIS...

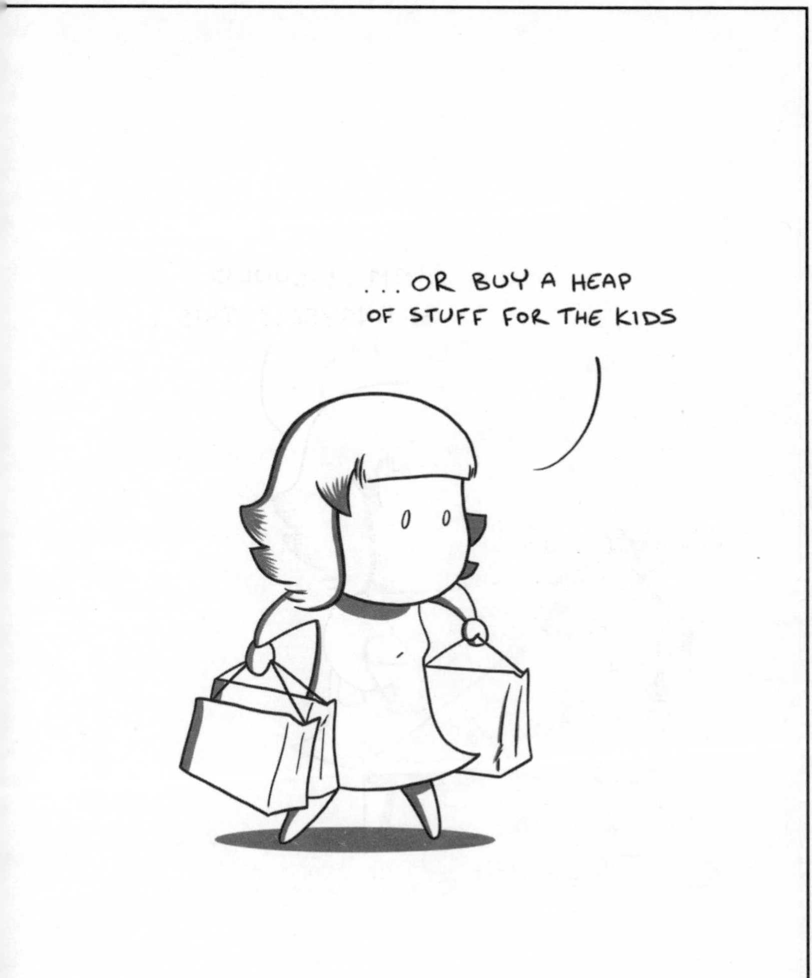
...OR BUY A HEAP
OF STUFF FOR THE KIDS

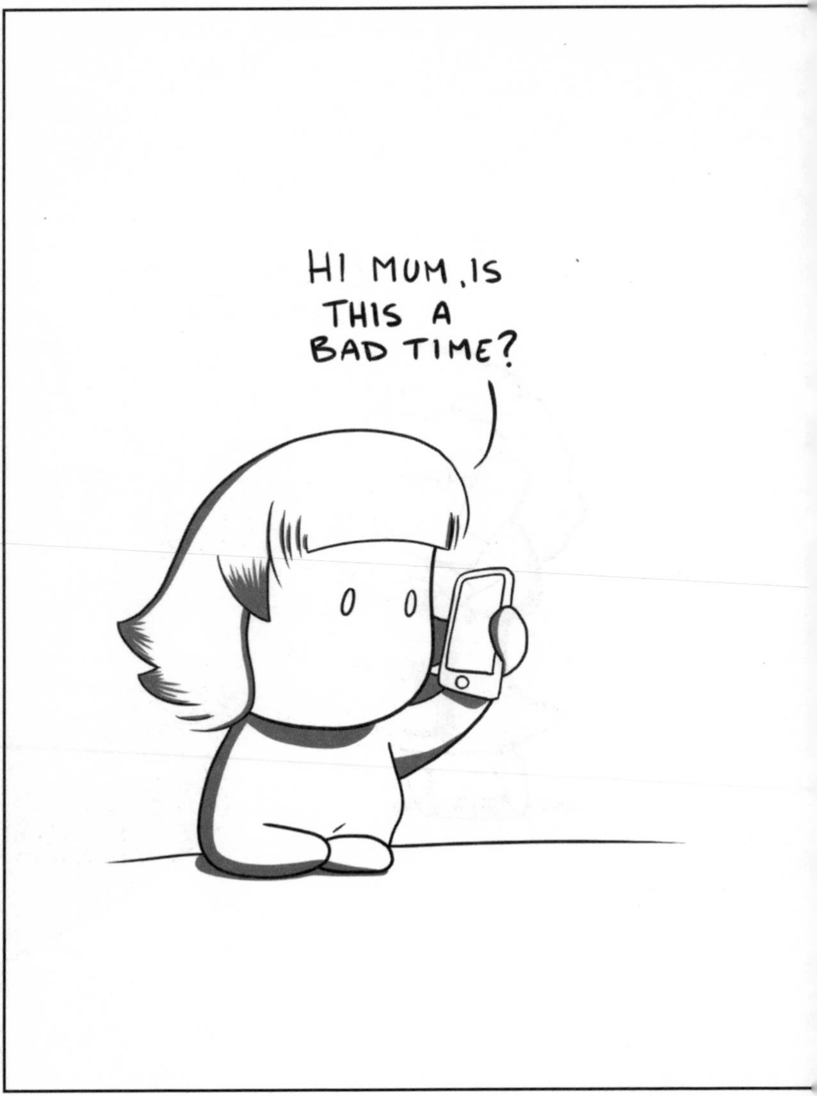
HI MUM, IS THIS A BAD TIME?

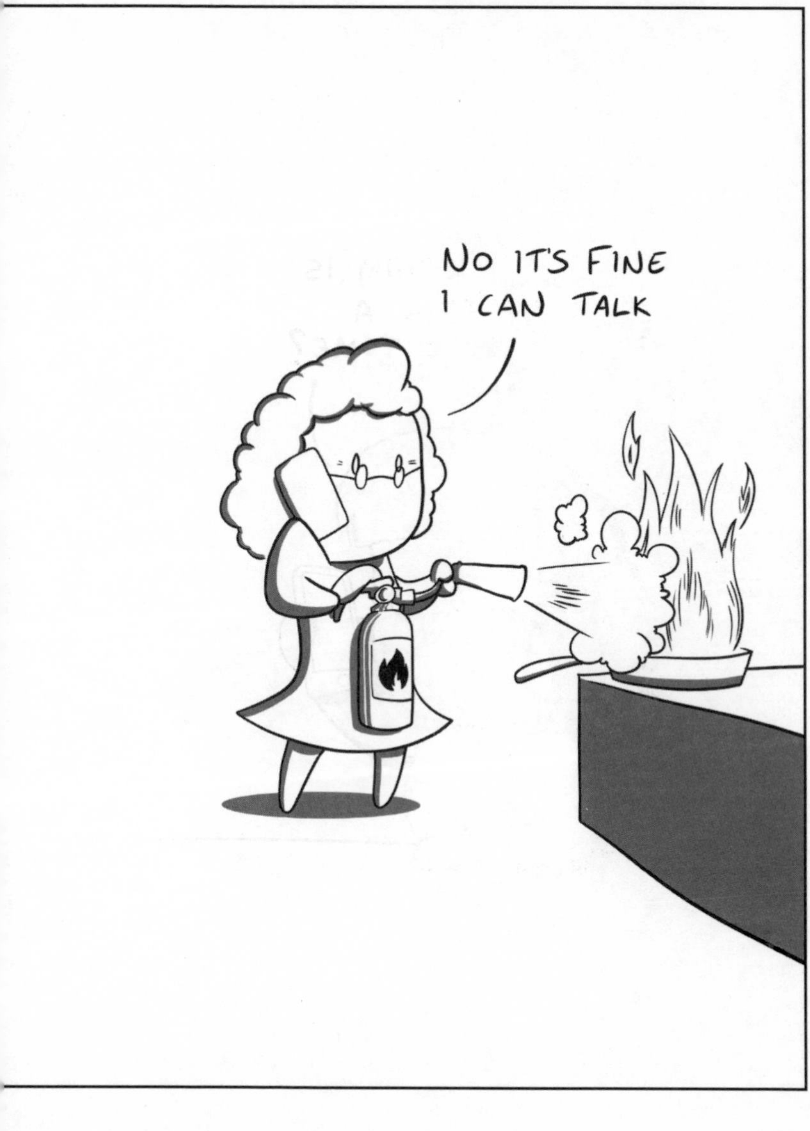
NO IT'S FINE
I CAN TALK

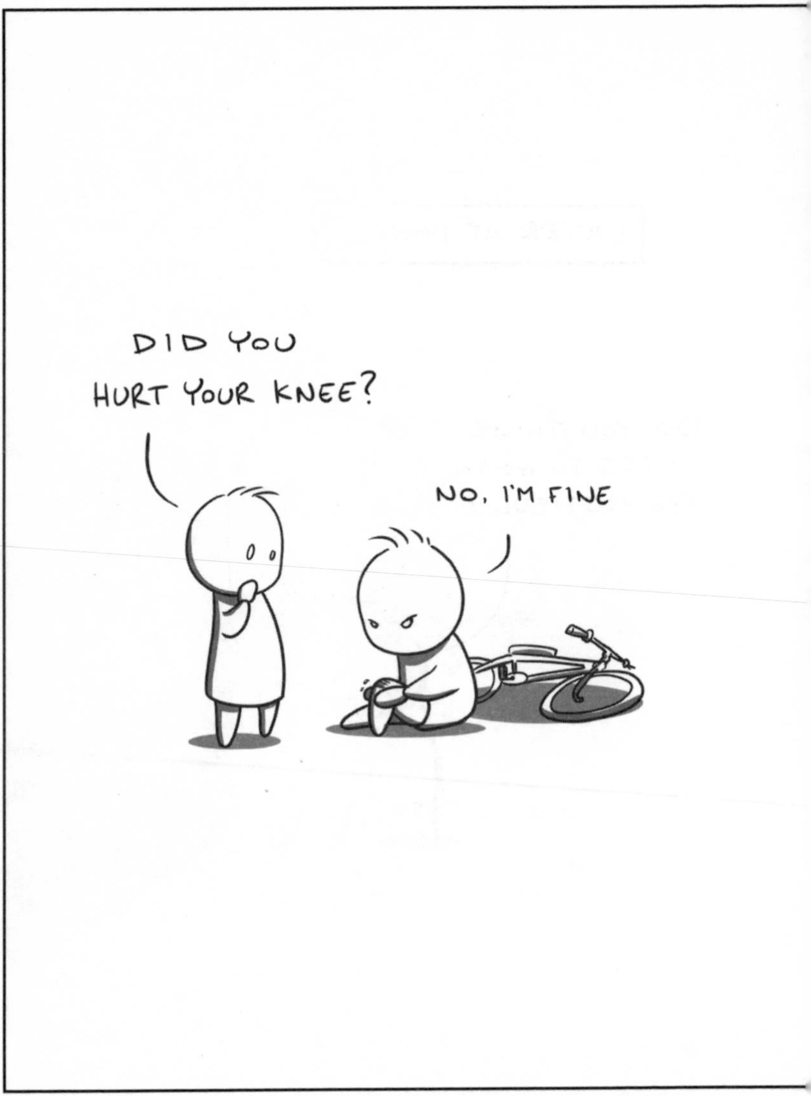
DID YOU
HURT YOUR KNEE?
NO, I'M FINE

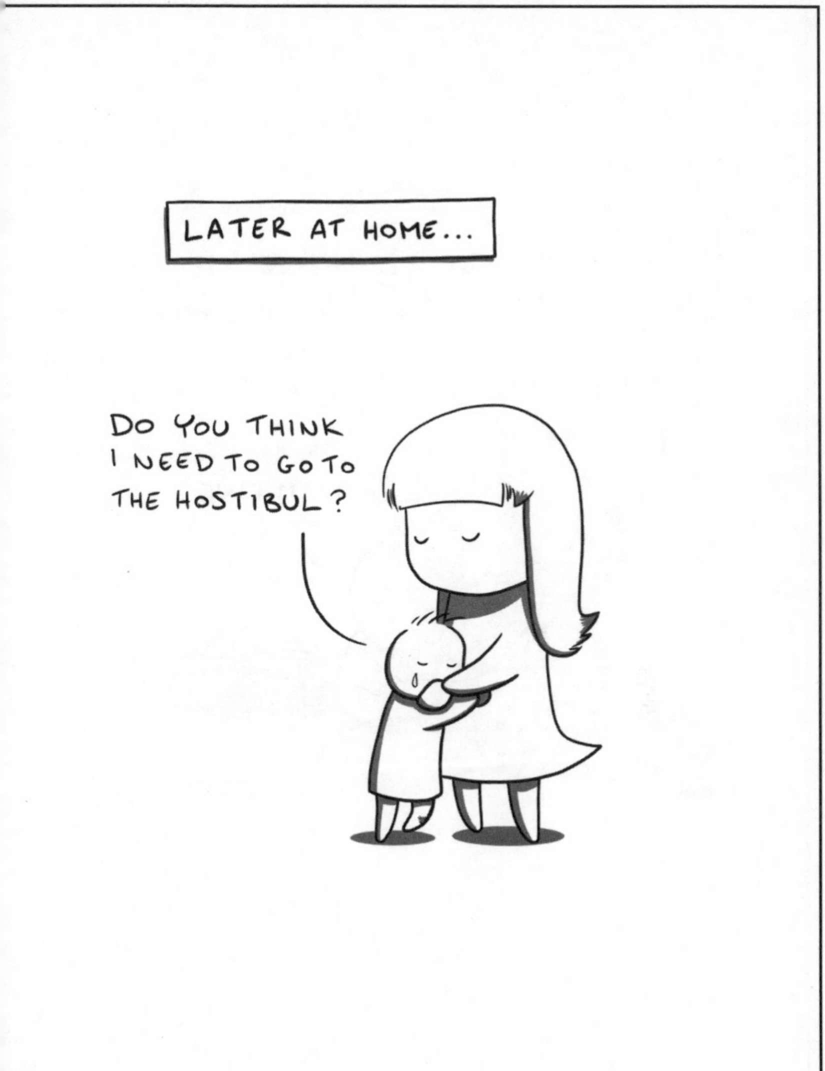
LATER AT HOME...
DO YOU THINK I NEED TO GO TO THE HOSTIBUL?

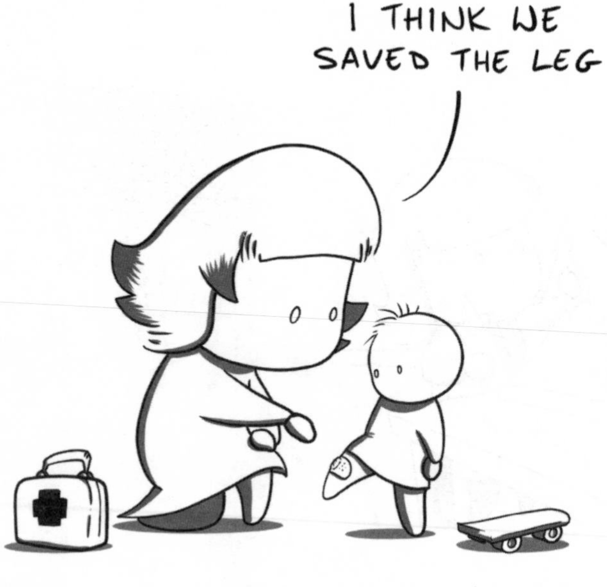
I THINK WE
SAVED THE LEG

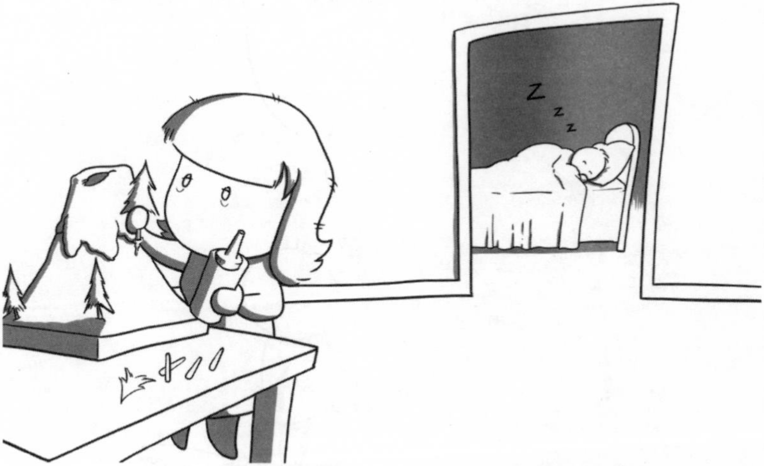
Z
Z
Z

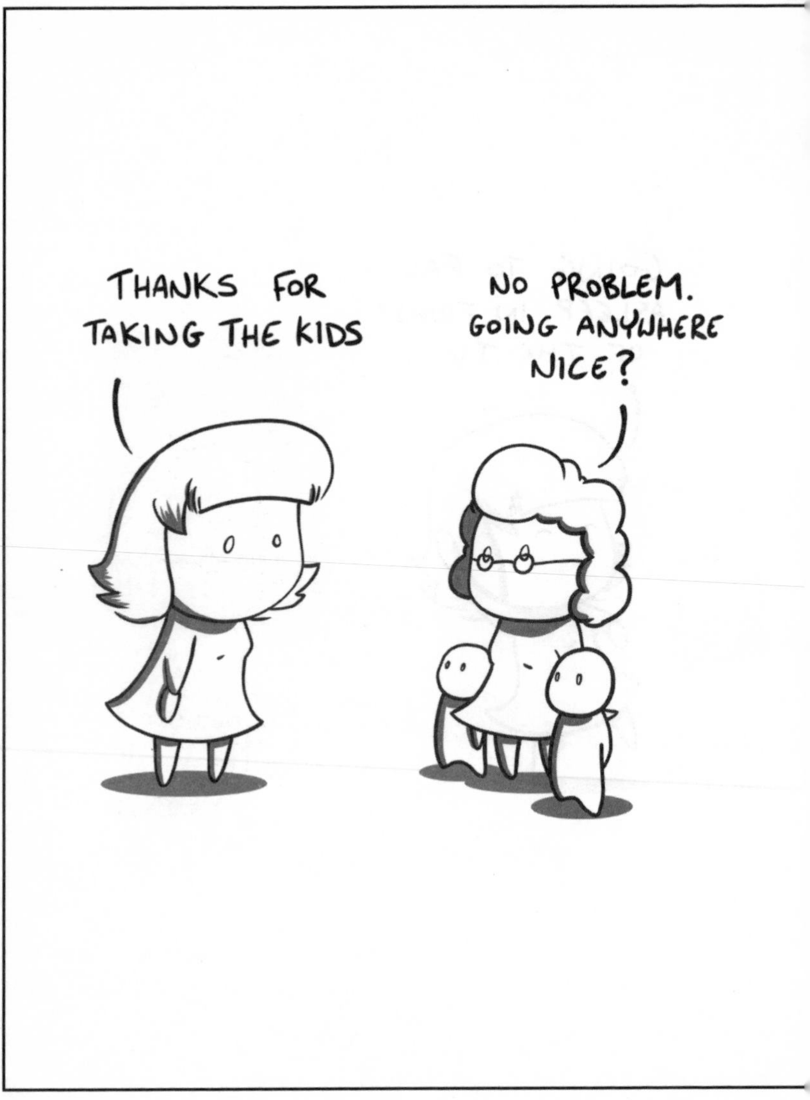
THANKS FOR TAKING THE KIDS
NO PROBLEM. GOING ANYWHERE NICE?

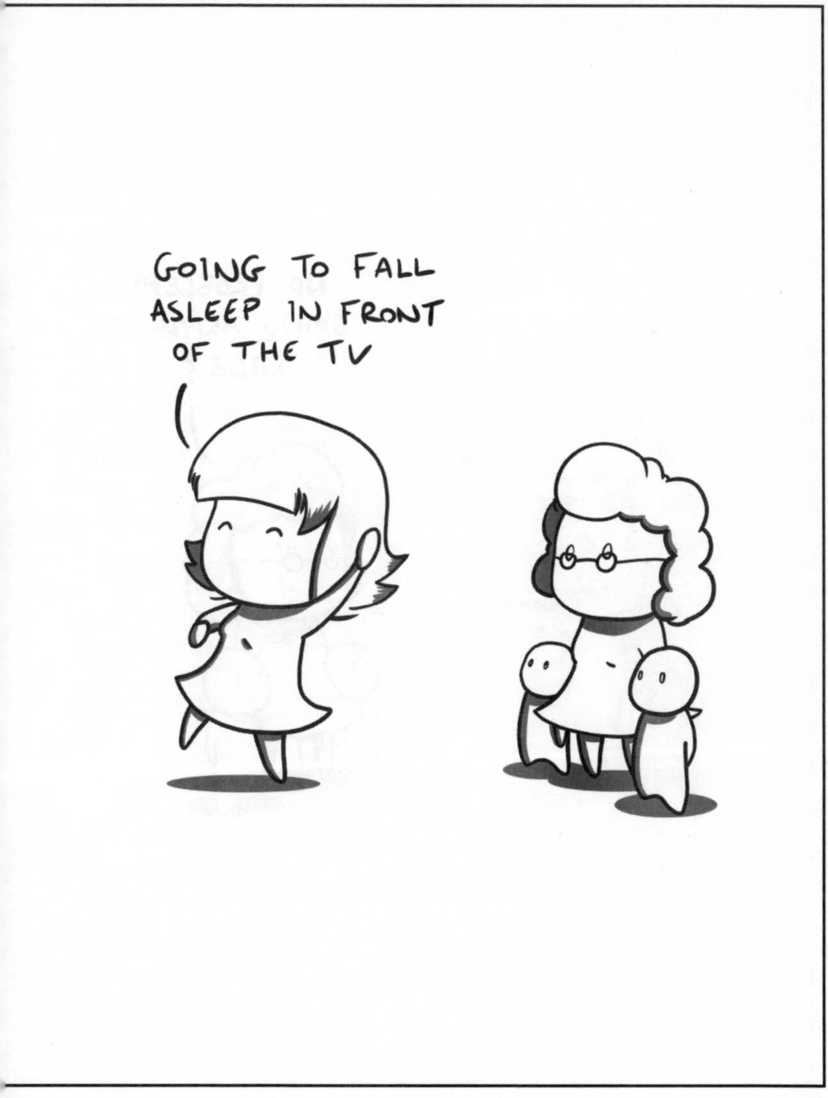
GOING TO FALL ASLEEP IN FRONT OF THE TV

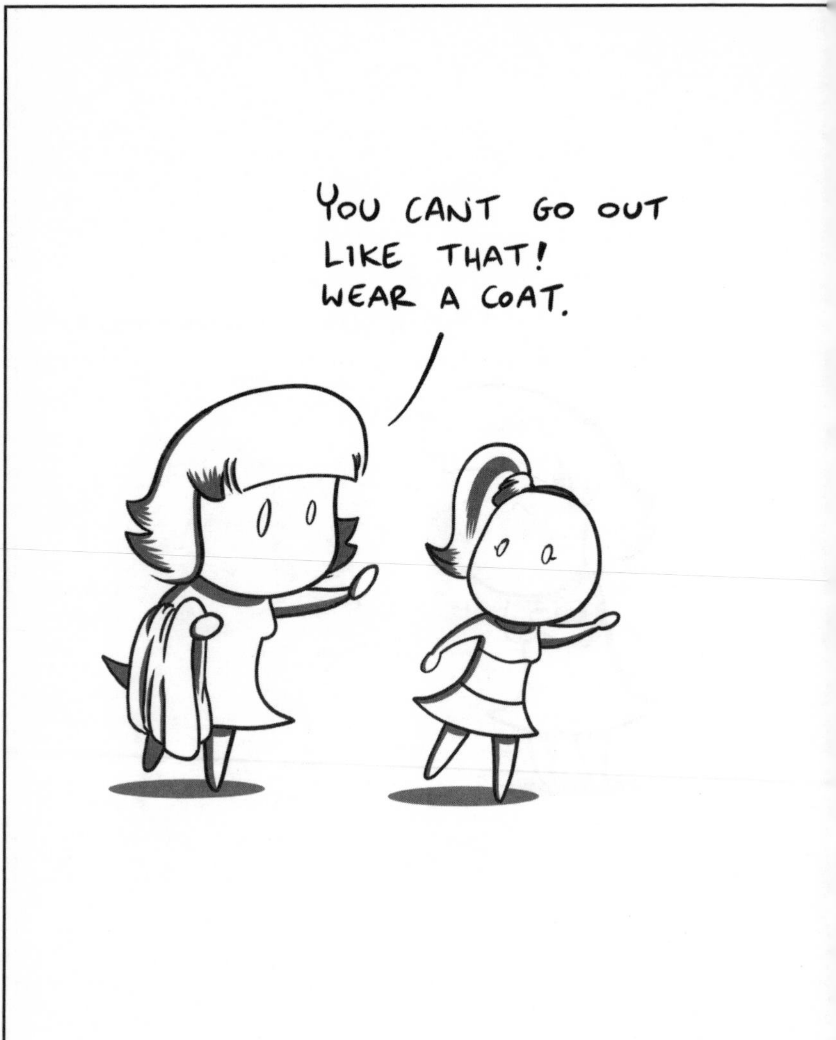
YOU CAN'T GO OUT LIKE THAT! WEAR A COAT.

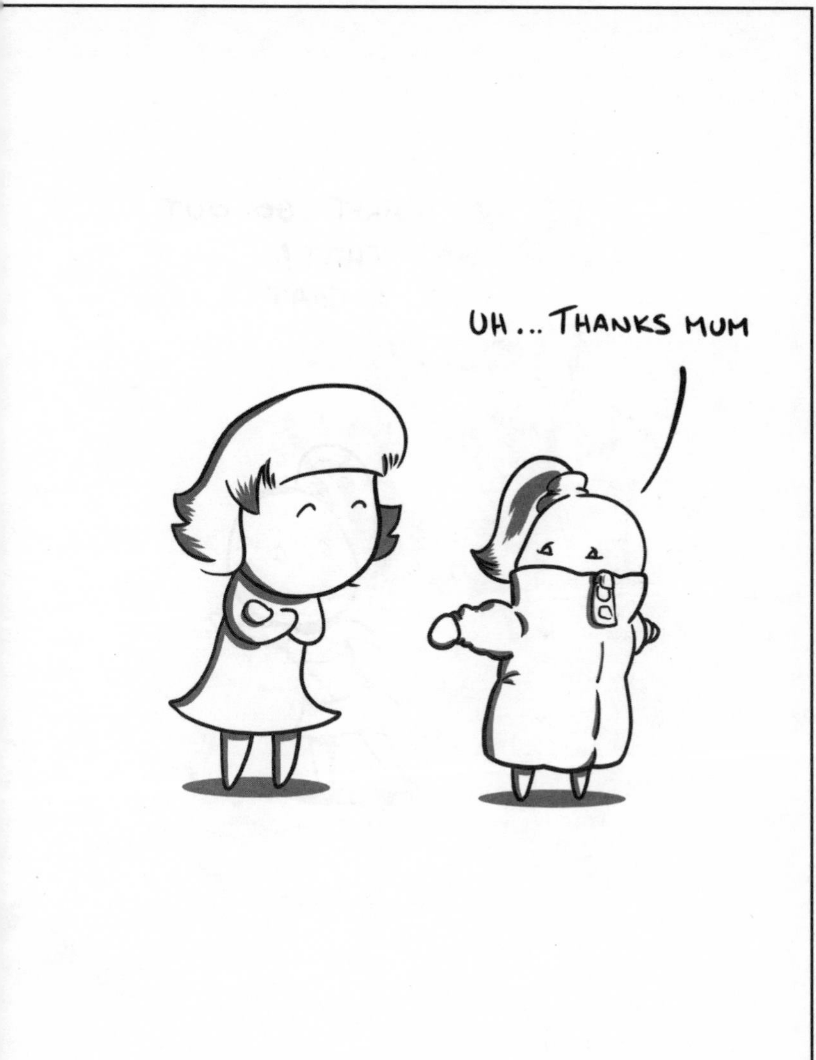
UH... THANKS MUM

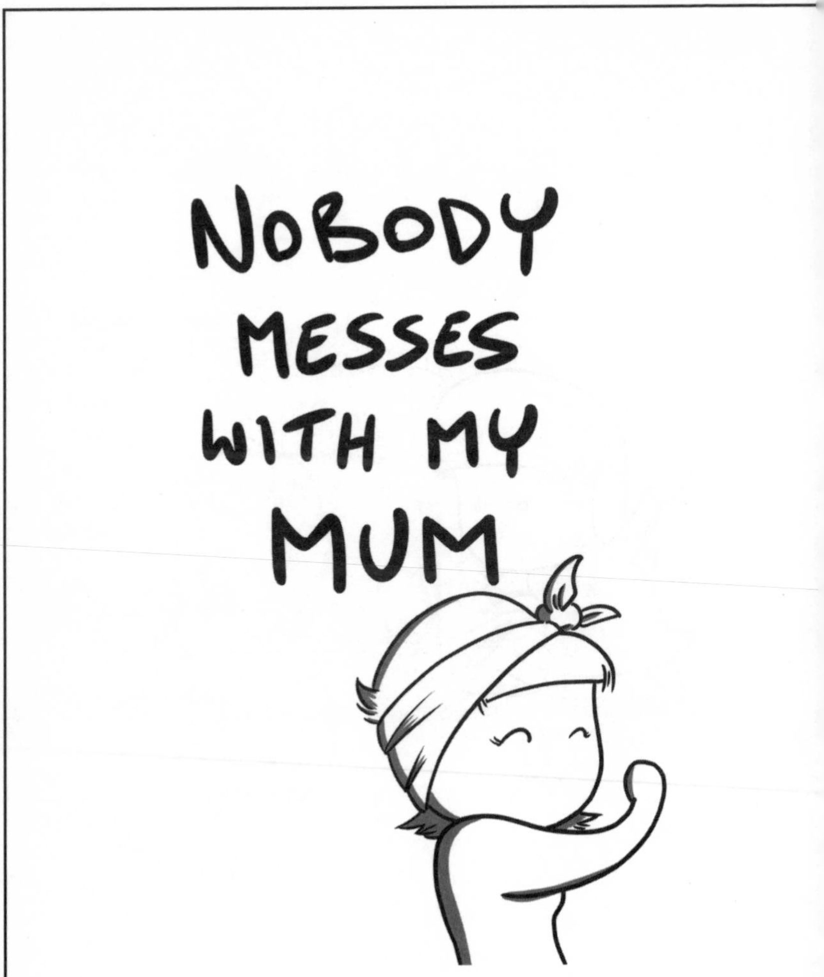
NOBODY MESSES WITH MY MUM

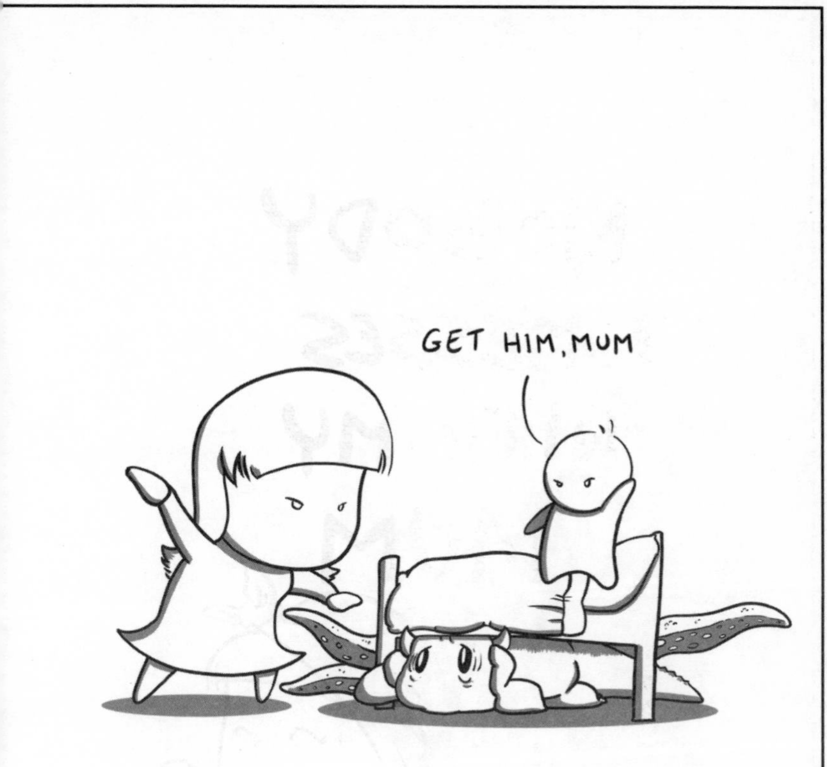
GET HIM, MUM

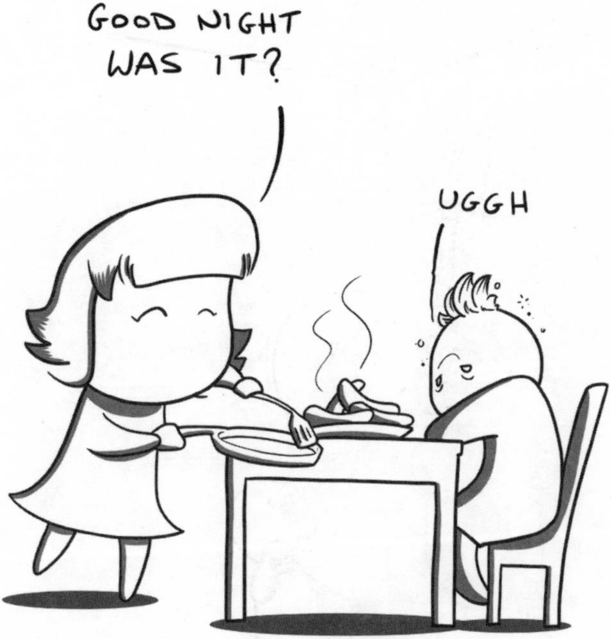
GOOD NIGHT WAS IT?
UGGH

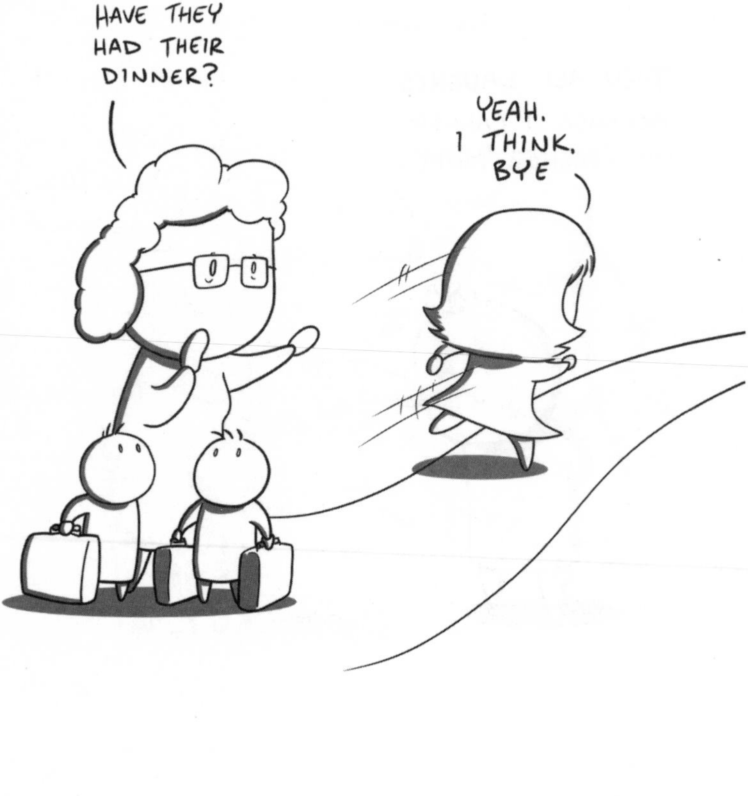
HAVE THEY HAD THEIR DINNER?
YEAH. I THINK. BYE

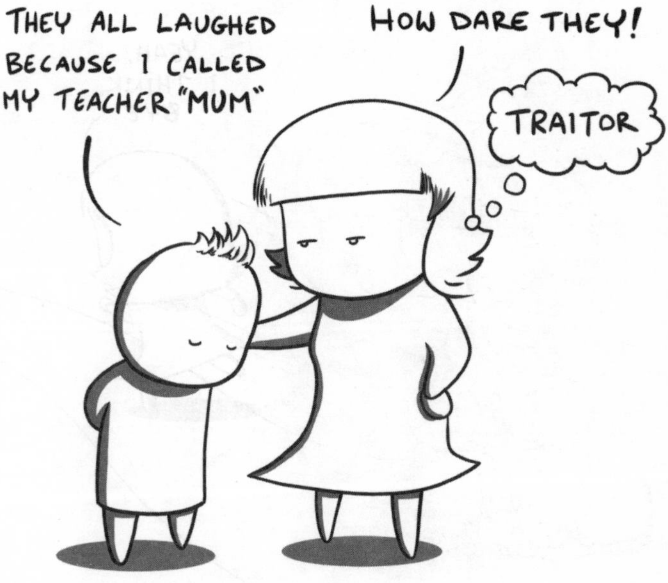
THEY ALL LAUGHED BECAUSE I CALLED MY TEACHER "MUM"
HOW DARE THEY!
TRAITOR

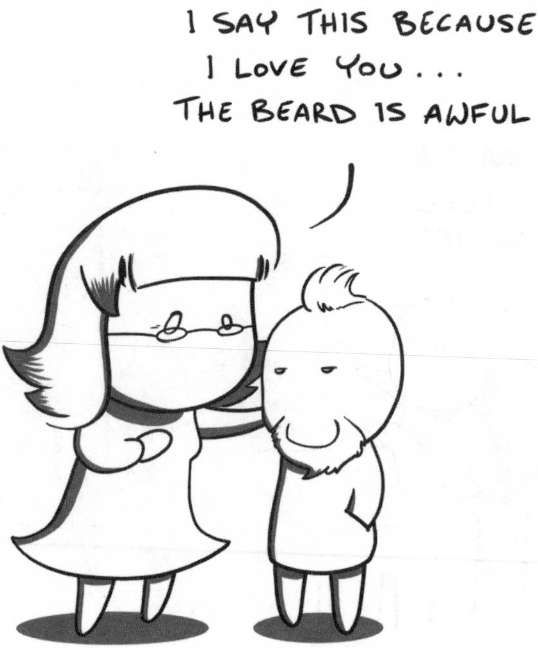
I SAY THIS BECAUSE
I LOVE YOU...
THE BEARD IS AWFUL

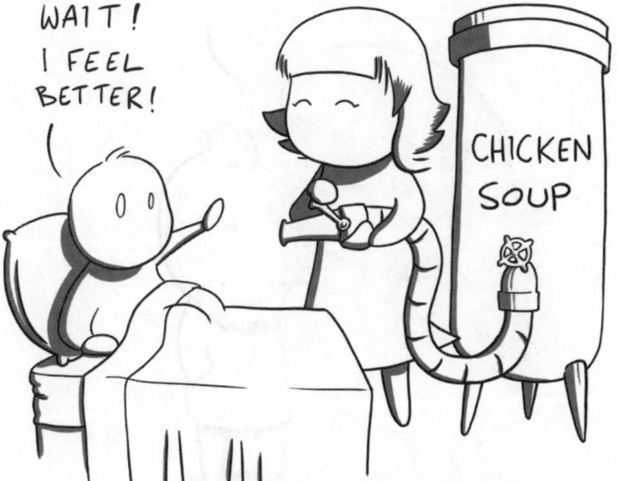
WAIT!
I FEEL
BETTER!
CHICKEN
SOUP

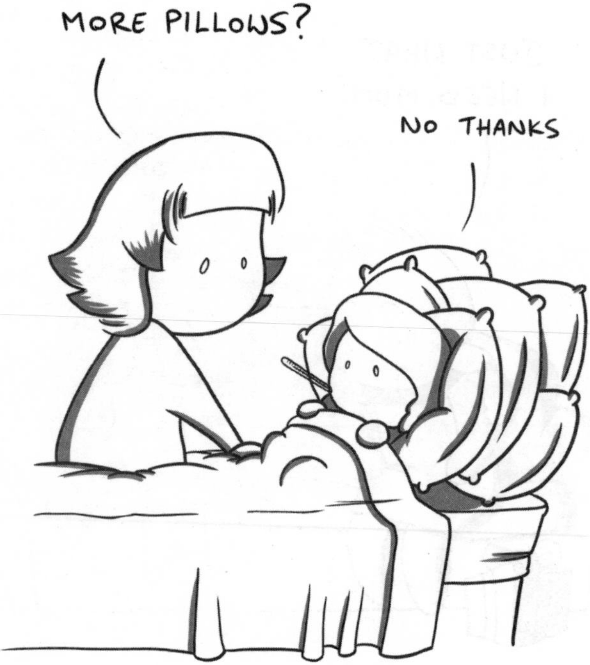
MORE PILLOWS?
NO THANKS

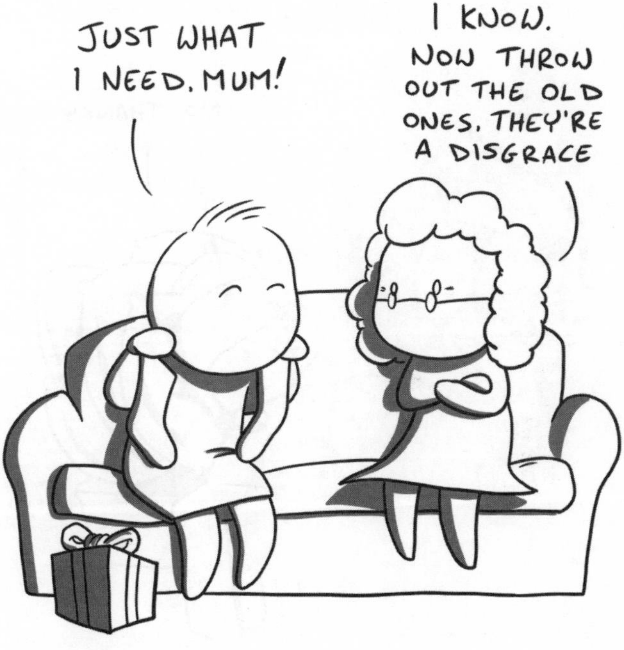
JUST WHAT I NEED, MUM!
I KNOW. NOW THROW OUT THE OLD ONES. THEY'RE A DISGRACE

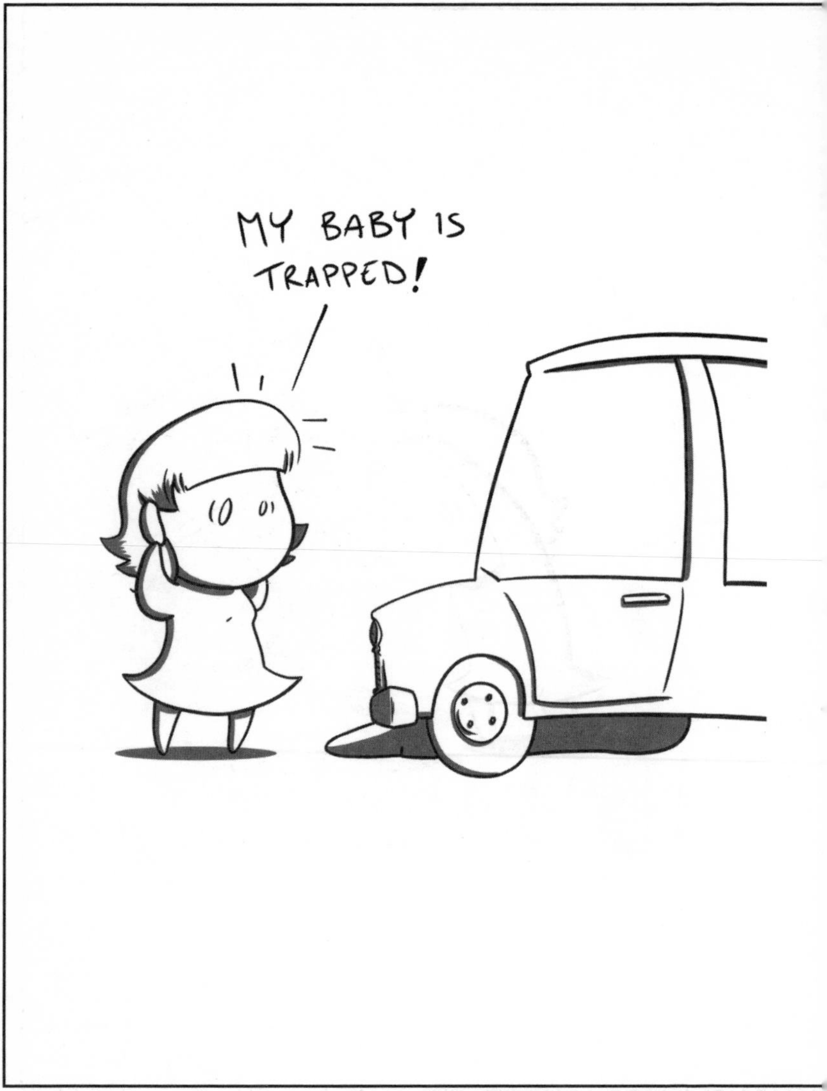
MY BABY IS TRAPPED!

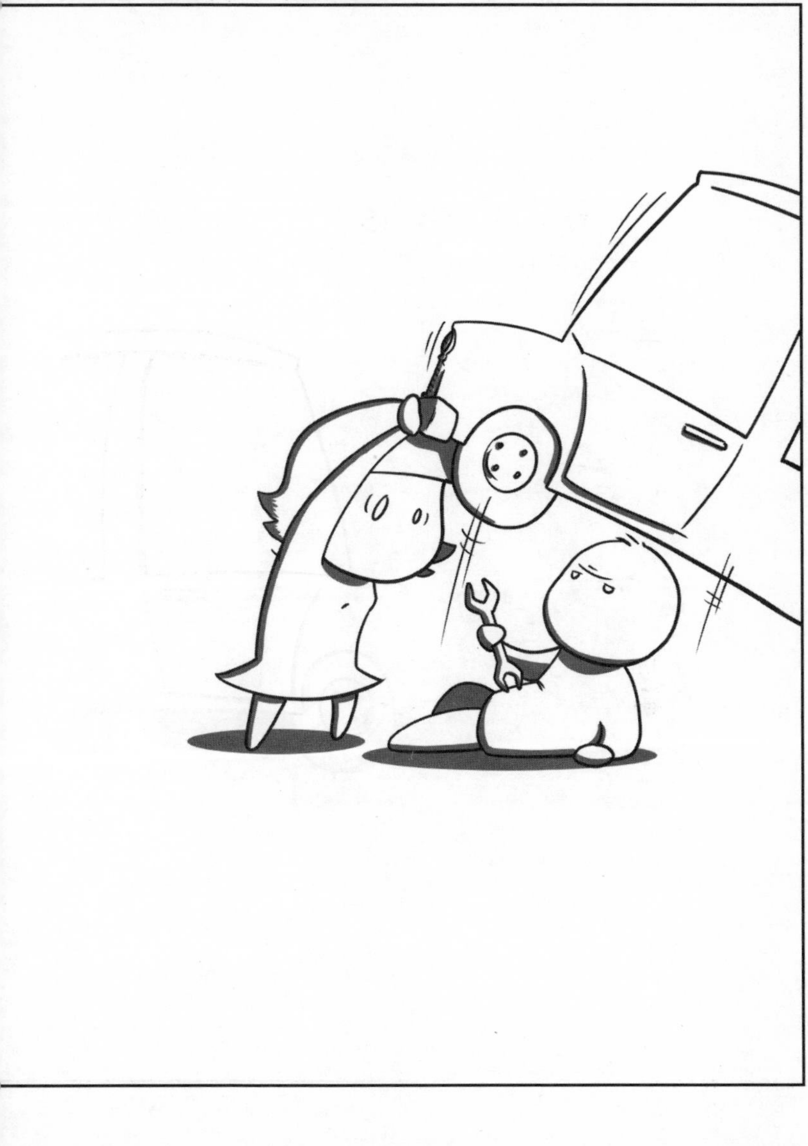

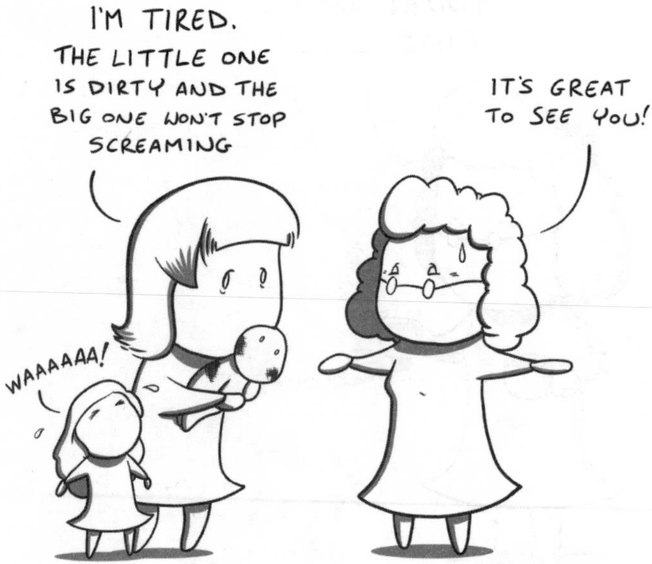
I'M TIRED.
THE LITTLE ONE IS DIRTY AND THE BIG ONE WON'T STOP SCREAMING
IT'S GREAT TO SEE YOU!
WAAAAAA!

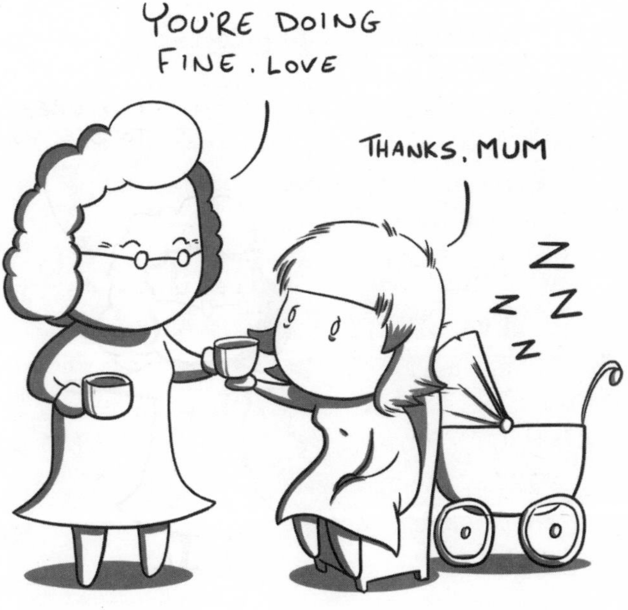
YOU'RE DOING FINE. LOVE
THANKS. MUM
Z Z Z Z

ACKNOWLEDGEMENTS

THANKS TO ALL AT HACHETTE PARTICULARLY CIARA CONSIDINE AND CIARA DOORLEY FOR HELPING TO DEVELOP THE ILLUSTRATION IDEAS FOR THIS BOOK.

THANKS AND LOVE TO MY WIFE ANNE WHO HAS TAUGHT ME MORE ABOUT MOTHERHOOD THAN I NEED TO KNOW.

AND LOVE TO MY OWN MOTHER WHO GOES BY "MAM".

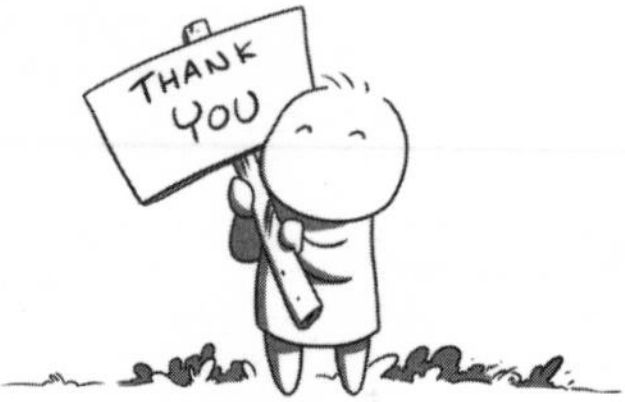

THANK YOU